HANK REINHARDT'S
Book of
Knives

BAEN BOOKS by HANK REINHARDT

The Book of Swords

Hank Reinhardt's Book of Knives with Greg Phillips

HANK REINHARDT'S
Book of Knives

A Practical and Illustrated Guide to Knife Fighting

by HANK REINHARDT
with GREG PHILLIPS

HANK REINHARDT'S BOOK OF KNIVES:
A Practical and Illustrated Guide to Knife Fighting

Copyright © 2012 by The Estate of Julius H. Reinhardt

Cover photography by Oleg Volk; interior illustrations by Dave Newton from originals by Allen Williams, art director, except as indicated; photographs of HRC items by Suzanne Hughes unless otherwise indicated; all other interior photographs as indicated; used by permission of the artists.

Neither the authors nor the publisher assumes any responsibility for the use or misuse of information contained in this book.

A Baen Books Original

Baen Publishing Enterprises
P.O. Box 1403
Riverdale, NY 10471
www.baen.com

ISBN: 978-1-4516-3755-7

First printing, June 2012

Distributed by Simon & Schuster
1230 Avenue of the Americas
New York, NY 10020

Library of Congress Cataloging-in-Publication Data

Reinhardt, Hank, 1934–2007.
  Hank Reinhardt's book of knives : a practical and illustrated guide to knife fighting / by Hank Reinhardt with Greg Phillips.
      p. cm.
  Includes bibliographical references and index.
  ISBN 978-1-4516-3755-7 (trade pb : alk. paper)
  1. Knife fighting. I. Phillips, Greg. II. Title.
  GV1150.7.R45 2012
  796.8—dc23

                                                        2012011495

10 9 8 7 6 5 4 3 2 1

Pages by Joy Freeman (www.pagesbyjoy.com)
Printed in the United States of America

Contents

Contents

PREFACE

Hank Reinhardt and I met, as best I can recall, in the early 1980s. I was a state trooper from up in Michigan, and had served with the Michigan State Police since turning twenty. With six years in the outfit, I had just transferred to my fourth post after serving a hitch in Detroit. I had my share of service awards, and I knew my business pretty well, even if I occasionally had to be the one who said so.

Hank was the instructor of a Knife/Counter-knife course he had devised for Mas Ayoob's Lethal Force Institute. Although MSP had taught me some rudimentary knife disarming, the general counter-knife protocol seemed to be, "If somebody is foolish enough to draw a knife on a policeman, he should be enthusiastically shot to pieces." Prevailing theory at that time held that in order to successfully defend against knives, a person should first learn how to use them. My patrol partner and I took personal leave and spent our own money to obtain the knife training Hank offered.

It would prove to be the smartest money I have ever spent, before or since.

It's safe to say that I had rather a high opinion of myself when first I encountered Julius Henry a.k.a. "Hank" Reinhardt. He was, I noted, a solidly built broad-shouldered man, somewhere near six feet tall, with smooth sun-browned skin and thick glasses, though he rarely saw fit to use them. What hair he had tended toward gray, and he spoke, walked, and gestured so slowly that I thought you'd have to set pins to see whether he was moving. I attributed his apparent sluggishness to his somewhat advanced years—the poor old gent was, after all, nearly twenty years my senior. I was smart enough to pick up the obvious thickness of his wrists, hands, and neck, which I recognized as good indicators of physical strength, even in men as old as he had managed to get.

Hank and I began verbally sparring immediately upon meeting at his home in Atlanta, Georgia. When he asked whether any of the dozen or so men attending the class had questions or comments before training began, I commented that the hand-written maps he had provided were pathetic, and added that I had seen clearer drawings on bathroom walls. Hank considered that observation, peered at me suspiciously, and asked, "You're a Yankee, aren't you?" I admitted I was, and he allowed that I was probably an authority on whatever is written on bathroom walls, then suggested that the others in the class make allowances for my whining because "Yankees get lost and confused real easy." When I mentioned that General Sherman certainly did a job of locating Atlanta some time before, I was gifted with a maddeningly disconcerting, carnivorous Hank smile. "You're a cold, cold man," he noted. "We're gonna get along just fine."

We were issued dummy knives, paired off, and began sparring. Hank demonstrated some basic moves that were different than I had seen before, then moved among the

Knife class. Hank Reinhardt, bottom row, second from right.
Mike Stamm, top row, farthest right. Massad Ayoob,
top row, farthest left. Photo by Richard Garrison

students offering suggestions and casually sparring with each
person. He gripped his knife with his thumb and his first two
fingers, as a skilled carpenter does his hammer. He snapped
the blade outward with blurring speed, striking any part of
his opponent's body within his reach. It seemed that just
about everything was within Hank's reach. I couldn't help
but notice that he moved with a fluid economy that made
him seem to glide toward his targets, and I also observed
that he didn't seem to be getting touched with anyone else's
blade. I began to regret having taunted him and sincerely
wished I had not mentioned General Sherman at all.

It was my turn to square off against unscathed Hank. As
my Dad would have summed it up, "School was in session."

I never touched the man. He was there, and then he wasn't.
When I struck at him, he moved *just* out of my reach. When
I attempted to recover, he literally sliced through my defenses
with impunity. Attempting to anticipate his movements only

resulted in blundering that left me even more open to his apparently effortless counters. The only way I could have possibly touched him would be to charge forward suicidally and hope that my momentum might draw some of his blood. It was beginning to seem like a fair trade.

I was gasping for air like a fish, while Hank hadn't bothered to break a sweat. I hoped to goad him into angry clumsiness, and said, "You move well for a man of your age." I received another wolfish Hank smile. "You do quite well," he allowed. "For a Yankee."

I spent the remainder of the weekend following Hank around like a puppy, pelting him with questions and scribbling down his patient and thoughtful responses. He was one of those rare individuals whose knowledge was vast and deep, and over the decades of our friendship I never found any subject that he could not discuss with passion and insight. He understood the mental and physical aspects of personal combat, and although he was astonishingly skilled at anything he sought to learn, Hank never boasted. His abilities were so apparent, he simply didn't have to. He knew more about battle implements of all types and origins than I would have believed possible, and he would share any knowledge he possessed with anyone who asked him. He balked at being called an expert in edged weaponry and its uses, as he considered himself "a student."

If you, too, are a student of knives, you will enjoy and benefit from Hank's work. Thankfully, he wrote just as he spoke, and when I read Hank's words I can honestly hear his deep clear voice with an aching clarity that reminds me how much I miss his wisdom and humor.

Hank Reinhardt knew knives, and you'll not go wrong listening to his advice.

—Mike Stamm, 2011

EDITOR'S NOTE

As with Hank Reinhardt's *Book of Swords*, this volume is being published posthumously. In the case of the former, it was because Hank died before putting the final polish on the manuscript he had been working on for two decades. In the case of this book, it was because he felt very ambivalent about making this material public.

Hank studied fighting in all its forms, from wrestling to rhetoric. He was probably the world's foremost authority on fighting with historical bladed weapons at the time of his death in 2007. But necessarily his understanding of swordplay and use of polearms was from recreation, not actual use in wars or duels. The same cannot be said of his understanding of fighting with knives.

Hank grew up in a large city (Atlanta) in the 1940s and '50s, and did not lead a life of suburban insulation. As a young man he got into fights, and he got into trouble, and the lessons imparted in this book come from his practical

Hank and his knives.
Photo by Richard Garrison

experience, his observations of fights, as well as decades afterward spent sparring, researching and thinking about bladed weapons. He wasn't precisely ashamed of his experiences, but he also knew they were not the sort of thing a gentleman bragged about, and Hank was always a gentleman. As he says, the best way to win a knife fight is to not be in one, and he certainly didn't want a book of his to encourage anything otherwise. From Chapter 2: "There has never been anything glamorous or heroic about it. It has always been a quick and dirty business and it always will be." And Chapter 6: "The real knife fighter does not wish to engage in a fight."

So he never tried to have the book published in his lifetime. It is for exactly this reason that we think what he had to say is important to the field, and we wanted to share that with more than just his actually rather large circle of friends. You, the reader, know that he has no ax to grind and that he is not trying to sell you seminars, videos, or super secrets of the samurai. He just put down the things about fighting with knives he thought it important to know. Besides, if any of these stories about people Hank knew happen to actually be about Hank, surely the statute of limitations has passed, and they can't catch him now.

The manuscript itself was written, we think, in the late 1970s, early 1980s. Bill Adams, Hank's partner at Museum Replicas, Ltd., the ground-breaking sword and bladed weapons catalog, helped Hank get the manuscript professionally typed. Sometime before the typing, an interior page was lost. Sometime in between that time and when Hank passed away in 2007 and I found the manuscript in his files, the first page of the manuscript went missing.

Rather than try to recreate the first page from context, we merged his short introduction with the first chapter. Added transitional material provided by Hank's student Whit Williams is indicated by brackets. Whit also had the

Hank at Dragoncon. Photo by Nils Onsager

idea of including more of Hank's students in this book and surveying them about what their best "lesson learned" from Hank was, and these responses are included in the "Interlude" between Parts I and II.

Another of Hank's students, Greg Phillips, wrote Part II, providing additional material updating the description of knives currently commercially available, and setting down more about Hank's training and sparring techniques. Greg worked with Hank for forty years learning about the history and performance of edged weapons, modern, medieval, and ancient. And he has been a security guard for decades, sometimes in the course of his duties putting into practice Hank's teachings. I can attest that he is also a great teacher in his own right.

When I use the word "student," I mean both those like Mike Stamm who took a formal course with Hank, and others, like Greg and Whit, whom Hank took under his wing and sparred with informally for many years. Hank made no distinction himself. If you were interested in bladed weapons, Hank would be happy to talk to you. (Or if you were interested in science fiction pulp magazines, or Gilbert and Sullivan, or bonsai trees, or WWI airplanes—but his thoughts on those topics will never be written down beyond what is archived at his website, www.hankreinhardt.com.)

Hank was a natural teacher. When we first started dating, he decided that since I was an editor of science fiction and fantasy I should know more about realistic fight techniques. Now, I've been carrying a knife since I was in first grade, sometimes a simple folder, but more usually a utility knife like a Leatherman or Swiss army multi-tool, so I agreed that my knowledge on fighting with knives could be expanded. He rolled up a piece of paper, handed it to me and told me it was a knife. He made one for himself and called on me to defend myself. Then he promptly gave me a paper cut. (I married him anyway.)

We hope that in this book you will experience something of what it was like talking with Hank and even, to some extent, sparring with him. Many of the illustrations are based on sparring sessions with him that were filmed, and the illustrations of positions and moves taken directly from the videos. Whit Williams, leader of the Reinhardt Legacy Fight Team, a group of men—many of whom were taught by Hank—who demonstrate and teach historical weapons use, and his brother Allen Williams, organized all the illustrations for this volume. Allen also provided the sketches for all of the drawings provided by illustrator Dave Newton. Most of the knives photographed for this volume belonged to Hank.

I can't say that I never saw Hank without a knife, but I can say that I never saw Hank with his clothes on without a knife. He was not a collector of knives as he was a collector of swords, polearms, kukris, and Indo-Persian arms and armor. He was an *accumulator* of knives, though, and had somewhere in the range of a hundred of various kinds when

he died. Some are functional works of art, like the Damascus
Jimmy Fikes Bowie knife illustrated within, some are historical European daggers, some exotic Eastern push-knives,
some anonymous generic folders, some weird hybrids that
Hank had worked on himself, including one large fighting
knife that he cut down from a Chinese polearm. When Hank
didn't have an example in his collection that was appropriate
to illustrate the text, we have borrowed from other sources,
like the collection of Patrick Gibbs, and labeled accordingly.
Knives that come from Hank's collection are indicated with
"HRC" and a number.

Many people helped out with this book in various capacities,
from proof reading to fact checking, including his daughters,
Dana Gallagher and Cathy Reinhardt, and his friends: Hilliard
Gastfriend, Mike Stamm, Steve and Suzanne Hughes, Jerry &
Charlotte Proctor, Greg Phillips, Patrick Gibbs, Peter Fuller,
Allen Williams, Nils Onsager, Jimmy Fikes, Steve Shackleford,
Mike Janich, Rich Garrison, Happy Heatherly, John Maddox
Roberts, Massad Ayoob, artist Dave Newton, and finally the
members (and wives & girlfriends) of the Reinhardt Legacy
Fight Team (check out reinhardtlegacyfightteam.com for
their calendar of demonstrations). This book could not have
been produced without the beyond-the-call-of-duty actions
of typesetter and book designer Joy Freeman. Of course, the
responsibility for any failings in the text or in our attempts
to illustrate Hank's techniques, falls to me, the editor. Please
feel free to send comments to me at: toni@baen.com.

—Toni Weisskopf Reinhardt, 2011

HANK REINHARDT'S
Book of
Knives

PART I

1

THE WARM FACE OF HISTORY

We learn so much about the knife from history and prehistory that we perhaps take it for granted. Don't. It dates back to the Stone Age in time, and it is found all over the world. Even cultures too primitive to know and use the wheel have some form of the knife. Such widespread acceptance is pretty amazing when you think about it.

It's also one of the most useful tools man has. You'll find it not only in the hunter's camp, but in the kitchen,

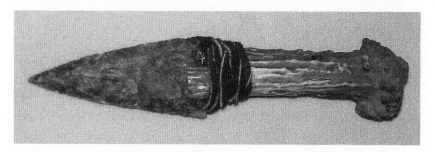

A flint knife made by Greg Phillips.
From the collection of Laura Brayman. Photo by Charlotte Proctor.

on the farm, in the garage, the home workshop—even in the artist's garret.

And every culture that has used it as a tool has also found uses for it as a weapon. A weapon is simply a tool for inflicting injury.

On the surface, the knife is a very simple device. Yet each society developed a knife or knives to its own individual needs and perceptions of what worked best. Thus the Gurkhas adopted and developed the kukri, the Arabs the jambiya, the Japanese the tanto. Most tribes and many individuals have developed slight variations on the theme of our very simple device.

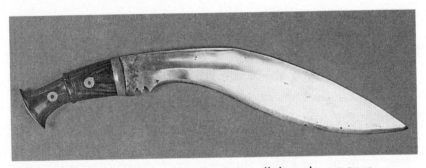

Nepalese kukri, 16 inches overall length. HRC545

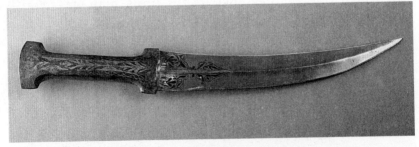

Arab jambiya, 15 inches overall length. HRC516

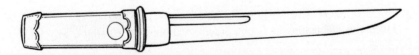

Japanese tantos are usually 12–14 inches overall length.

A good many factors can go into influencing the way a knife can be developed, including available materials and purpose. Over the years, style and fashion have played as important a role in the creation of knives as they have in the creation of clothing: a knife can very easily become a mere decorative accessory. It should also be remembered that knife fighting techniques frequently develop around the type of knife most readily available. Technique does not that often drive design of the knife.

Frankly, there are styles I just don't understand. One of them is the Ethiopian sword, the shotel, which is a long, deeply curved blade that is sharpened on the inside edge. It is not a chopping weapon like the kukri. Rather, it is used to reach around an opponent's shield and stick him. Now this is a good trick with a curved sword, but as a fighting style it is marvelously ineffective.*

A shotel.

Illustration by Peter Fuller.

[There are styles that did work, however, and some of them were recorded for posterity. One manual in particular I have always found useful, as it includes knives as well as swords. The style described in it cannot be called a] modern combat style, but it has captured the essence of the art, and done it very well.

The author of this work was George Silver, an English fencing master who lived in the late sixteenth century. He seems

---

* Editor's Note: this is where a page was missing from Hank's manuscript; his introduction is merged into his first chapter. The transitional material, shown in brackets, was written by Whit Williams.

to have been not only a Master of the Sword, but of practically every other edged weapon as well. He had a knack of grasping the capabilities and limitations of various weapons with little or no apparent effort. His book, *Paradoxes of Defense*, is an excellent assessment of many weapons, and in view of his fame with the sword, it's interesting that he preached the superiority of the "short sword" over the rapier. This was prophetic, as what he termed the "short sword" became known as the small sword or the dueling sword.

In the quotation below, I have modified the antiquated spelling for the purposes of clarity. But I want you to remember something as you read it. George Silver made his living with a sword, not with books.

First know that to this weapon there be no wards nor grips but move against such a one as if foolhardy and will suffer himself to have a full stab in the face or body to hazard the giving of another, then against him you may use your left hand in throwing him aside, or strike up his heels after you have stabbed him.

In this dagger fight you must use continual motion so that he not be able to put you too close to grips, because your continual motion disappoints him of his true place, and the more fierce he is in running in, the sooner in giving you the place, whereby he is wounded and you not endangered.

The manner of handling your weapon and continual motion is this. Keep out of distance and strike or thrust at his hand, arms, face or body. Press upon him, and if he defends the blow or thrusts with his dagger, make your blow or thrust at his head.

If he comes in with his left leg forwards, or with the right, do you strike at him as soon as it shall be within your reach, remembering to use continual motion in your progression and regression.

Although the dagger fight be thought a very dangerous fight by reason of the shortness and singleness of the weapons, yet the fight being handled as aforementioned is as fast, safe and defensive as any other. Thus endeth my brief instructions.

Street fighting and knives are not generally considered pleasant subjects. They seem to generate a certain distaste and scorn. Oddly enough, this scorn frequently occurs in the sort of people who extol the virtues of Jim Bowie and man-to-man shoot-outs in the Old West. The knife fights of Jim Bowie are the stuff of legends and the man-to-man shoot-outs of the Old West are questioned by many historians. No matter. Those things happened a long time ago.

Street fights with the knife still occur.

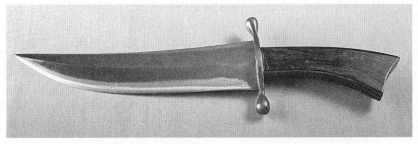

Hank's experimental double-edged fighting knife, 13 inches overall length. HRC43

2

THE COLD EYE OF REALITY

Knife fighting has often been held to be somewhat glamorous, even heroic. Here's your first, and one of the most important lessons in the science: Hogwash.

There has never been anything glamorous or heroic about it. It has always been a quick and dirty business and it always will be. When two men are facing each other with death as the very probable outcome, the only thing that counts is surviving. With that as the goal, most people choose to throw everything else out the window.

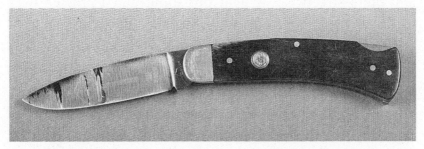

Standard folder, 7¾ inches overall length. HRC617

Here's your second and even more important lesson about the science of knife fights: stay out of them. If you can run, run. If you can't run, shoot. If you don't have a gun and can't run, well, maybe what follows will be of help.

Let's start with one aspect of the knife fight that most, if not all the other books, have ignored: what happens afterward. Cutting and/or killing another human being is regarded in a rather serious light by our society. The courts take an especially dim view of knives and the use of them on other people. Punishment can be severe.

A friend of mine who is a cop told me about the first real cutting he ever saw (he doesn't count minor stabbings). Some guy went berserk in a bar and started slicing up people. One of his victims was cut so badly there was some question as to whether he would live. The knife wielder was lucky, however, in that someone brained him with a chair before the cops, including my friend, arrived. Had he still been standing then, he would quickly have received a chestful of .357s. Some great luck. Now all he has to worry about is being in jail, under $30,000 bond, facing three to five in the state prison. I wonder if he feels what set him off is worth what he's looking at now?

When I was about sixteen, I saw my first knife fight. I was, I admit, roaming a ghetto section of town where I had no real reason to be. I was just looking around, feeling tough and quite streetwise. A fight broke out and I crossed over to watch the action. This was great fun, then.

There were two guys in their early twenties. Both had knives out, but weren't circling or moving at all. Then they both moved forward and started slicing. No fancy moves, no dodging, no parrying, just two crazy guys hacking away at each other. It lasted about a minute, although to me it seemed like half an hour. Then one stepped back and you could see blood spurting from his neck. He shook his head slightly, then fell. The other walked forward holding his stomach. Then he turned and collapsed on the ground and you could see his entrails on the pavement.

They had tied for second place.

I never realized that two men could hold so much blood. By the time the ambulance arrived, they were both dead. I wondered at the time what it was they fought about. I still wonder. Was it worth their lives? It had better have been because that's what it cost them.

That was thirty years ago* and things were a little different then. Two guys could get into a fight, one or both get cut and, when the cops came, no one knew who did it. If one of them got caught, he'd claim he was jumped by a total stranger. If they both got caught, they'd claim they were both jumped by two other strangers. No one wanted the police in their quarrels.

I remember one guy who did call the cops, however.

He was a redheaded guy who worked out at the gym with us. When he started, he was pretty skinny, but he gained some weight and got right husky. Then he stopped coming. He failed to show up for workouts and no one heard from him. Finally, one night he walked in. He looked like death warmed over. He'd lost about twenty-five pounds. His head, neck and back were crosshatched with scars. I thought he had been in a wreck and gone through a windshield, but the lines were awfully straight.

After repeated questioning, he finally told us the story.

Seems he had got into a fight with a neighbor and as they started to square off, the other guy flicked out his knife. Red backed off and then popped out his own knife.

Red said that his neighbor stopped, threw down his knife and said, "Nah. Red, we been friends for too many years. Let's just have it out man to man. No knives."

---

* Thirty at the time of writing, sixty years at the time of first publication.

Red, being a gallant, if somewhat stupid, soul, agreed and threw down his knife, next to his neighbor's.

I didn't really need to ask what happened, but I did.

Red, looking somewhat embarrassed, said, "He reached down and picked up both of them."

I managed not to laugh, and then Red told me he'd done something really bad to get even.

"When I woke up in the hospital, I told the po-lice who it was that cut me, and even swore out one of them warrants. It may have been dirty, but he had no right to cut me with my own knife."

I lost touch with Red and haven't heard of him since. But I bet he owns a lot of land in Florida, and several bridges to boot.

I don't mean to be flippant about Red or his neighbor, but how anyone could be so innocent and grow up in the same neighborhood I did is beyond me. Once those knives are out, it's totally different from a high school fistfight. It is real and very, very serious. No games, no givebacks. It's for every marble, all at once. If you have a choice, don't play. It simply isn't worth it. If you don't have a choice, however, then play tough, hard, strong, and for keeps. Because it is for keeps.

But as I said, things have changed. Now you stand a very good chance of a long jail term. If I harp on that, bear with me. All too many people think once it's over, it's over. But it isn't. Frequently, a ten-second knife fight kicks off twenty years of grief.

Blood has never turned me on. I dislike it, mine or anyone else's. But given a preference, I would rather see his blood than mine, and that has to be your feeling, also. Being tough, able to take pain, etc., is fine. But is it intelligent?

It might surprise you to know how many people are fearful

of hurting someone else. This is well and good. Maybe it indicates these folks are a little higher up the evolutionary ladder than the rest of us. But in combat, whether it's on the street or a battlefield, that attitude will sign your death warrant.

Quick and dirty. Ugly and brutal. It's no game to take lightly. I admit I have known some who did and are now growing old peacefully, but I've known a far greater number

Wound, downward cut across the body.

who're not growing old at all. Or else are doing it behind bars.

Once you get involved, you're talking about the rest of your life. Just how lightly do you take the rest of your life?

3

THE STREET KNIFE

A lot of books have been written about fighting knives. They've discussed the Bowies, the Fairbairn-Sykes, the kukri—in short, the "glamour" knives. "Street" knives are usually dismissed in a short paragraph, if they're mentioned at all. This always

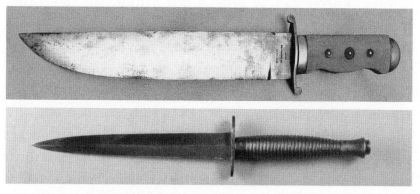

Top: A historic Bowie knife, 16 inches overall length.
From *The Antique Bowie Knife Book,* Norm Flayderman collection
Bottom: Reproduction Fairbairn-Sykes,
11½ inches overall length. HRC612

A typical folding pocket knife, 7¾ inches overall length. HRC616

struck me as odd, since there have probably been more people killed or injured with these knives than any other.

Fighting knives can be broken down into two categories. The large sheath knives that are worn openly and the smaller concealed weapon types. It is not my purpose to deal with fighting knives in general in this book, but only with the smaller types. The larger knives have a method of use that is all their own. Techniques that work with a full-sized blade will not work with a small knife. There is obviously some overlap, and no expert can tell you exactly where the cutoff in size lies. But there is enough of a difference to warrant a separate study and explanation.

Street knives can be broken down into two categories: the folder and the small sheath knife. Push daggers would fall into the latter category, although they are generally less versatile than any of the others.

Folders have always been the most prevalent and the reason is obvious. You might talk a judge or cop out of a concealed weapons charge if all you're carrying is a pocket knife. It's much harder to do that when you have a small dagger that is obviously intended only as a weapon. A folder is also cheaper and can be thrown away with much less of a financial loss.

The perennial favorite of the Hollywood Bad Guy is the switchblade. The movies were very successful in establishing this as the ultimate weapon of the juvenile delinquent. They were so successful, the things were banned and it's damned

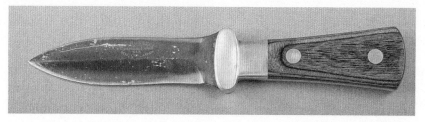

A small concealable boot knife, 6¾ inches overall length. HRC32

near impossible to find one nowadays. Knifings still continued at the same old pace and that should tell people something.

In the movies, Bad Guys always opened their knives with a very loud and menacing click. Now, this "click" has always impressed a certain type of knife carrier. He might not have an idea what to do with a knife, and he almost always would be better off if he could open the thing without attracting attention. But no. He wants the knife to produce a very loud click when it opens. It's the same type of mentality that judges a car by the way the door slams. The durn thing may not have much of a motor, but if the door closes with a solid thunk...

Ninety-nine percent of the switchblades I've seen were the edged-weapon version of the Saturday Night Special, not even worth the single buck they usually cost. Just cheap, poorly made pieces of junk. A few years after the end of the Second World War, some new switchblades appeared on the market. These were the Italian switchblade stilettos.

They were well-made knives with good springs, good riveting, and decent steel blades. But they suffered from two faults. The blades were meant only for stabbing and had an

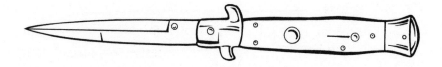

Italian switchblade stiletto.

edge too dull to be decently used for cutting. The second fault was that they were designed like many of the other switchblades with a button to open and a lock to keep the blade being pushed accidentally. That meant it opened too slowly. If you carried the knife with the lock on, you had to push it off before you pressed the button. By the time you did this, a fast man could thumb a manual folder open and cut you. The alternative was to carry your knife with the lock off and that was not wise, either.

I heard about one guy who was kissing a girl with a great deal of passion and she pressed against him. The knife sprang open in his pocket. So much for passion.

There was one switchblade available then that was quite excellent. It was a German knife sold in Army-Navy surplus stores. It didn't work on a button, but rather a lever that was hinged on the front bolster. By flipping the lever up and back quickly, you could cause the blade to spring out. The lever flipped back into position, locking the blade. It was made of good steel that would take a razor-sharp edge, and it had a strong spring. It wasn't popular, possibly because it didn't make much noise when it opened. I rather liked that, since I couldn't imagine many situations where I wanted to advertise I was opening a knife. But I've never been on the cutting-edge of fashion. It was the only type of switchblade I ever owned and it cost me $2.95. I ran across one in about 1979 and the price was a cool $100.00. I passed it up.

Most of the people I knew in my younger days carried a plain pocket knife. Usually they carried a Case, Queen,

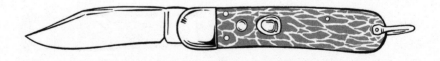

German switchblade with lever.

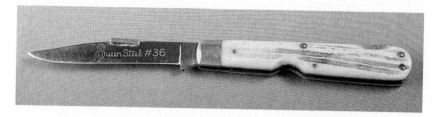

Hank's Queen, 8½ inches overall length. HRC650

Western, or Sabre. Lockbacks were prized, but very hard to find.

Lockbacks are knives where the blade locks into place once it is opened. The lock must be released before the blade can be closed. Usually this is done by pressing a spring on the back of the knife.

The fact that most knives did not lock led to a pretty good maneuver that was taught to me by a man who was at least sixty-five. I was seventeen. The move was simplicity itself: merely striking down with the open hand across the back of the blade held by your opponent. This caused the blade to close, cutting fingers when it was stopped by the hand. There was the simple and obvious counter of merely turning the knife so that the blade is edge up.

The old man explained it to me and I just didn't believe he could do it. I was considered pretty fast. I held a small

Striking down across the back of an opponent's blade causes the blade to close, cutting fingers when stopped by the hand.

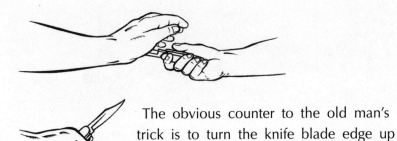

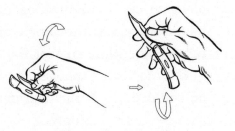

The obvious counter to the old man's trick is to turn the knife blade edge up

stick and I knew what he was going to do and he did it anyway. I felt like a spastic snail.

I've always had a lot of respect for old people because some of them didn't get that way by being timid. Some of them are just plain dangerous!

OPENING THE FOLDER

There are four basic ways to open a folder and we'll deal with each in turn.

Most knives have springs that allow them to be popped open with a quick flick of the wrist. The blade is gripped tightly between thumb and index finger, and the hand is then snapped downward and back. With a little practice, this can be done in the space of a few inches, barely moving the hand.

The folding knife can also be opened by reversing the grip and holding the handle

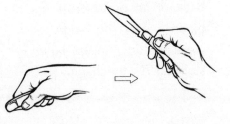

Popping open a folder by holding the blade (above) and by holding the handle (below).

Thumbing open a folder: start (left) to finish (right).

rather than the blade. This is harder to do because the blade has less mass than the handle. This also requires faster hand and arm movement and more room.

The most common method of opening a pocket knife was to thumb it. The knife is gripped by the thumb and middle finger with the pivot point of the knife (where the blade is hinged) pointing away. The little finger and the ring finger are on the sides of the knife handle. The thumb presses down and out, while the last two fingers pull back. This causes the blade to rotate forward into an open position. This operation can be sped up by snapping the wrist and imparting some momentum to the blade. This method involves a certain element of risk. If the thumb contacts the edge and moves along it, the result is a nasty cut. This is not only painful but it plays hell with the tough, macho image that should go along with the movement.

It is, however, possible to contact the edge with the thumb and not get cut. This requires that the thumb roll across the edge, exerting only a minimum amount of pressure and no forward movement at all. But it's tricky and I certainly don't advise trying it. Better to practice opening it with the thumb, putting pressure on the side of the blade and not contacting the edge.

One definite advantage to this style of opening is that it can be done quietly. By doing the movement slowly and gripping the knife very tightly, you can muffle the sound so that it can hardly be heard.

The third way to open a knife one-handed is also the easiest to master. Here, the knife is gripped by thumb and

index finger, but the pivot
point is jammed back against
the ball of the thumb. The
little finger is hooked on the
side of the knife and presses

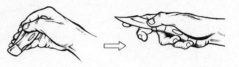

Third one-handed method.

down quickly. This can be done with no movement of the
hand at all, only the fingers. The only disadvantage is that the
knife must be shifted forward to get the hand off the blade.

Many of the people I've known to use this method also
ground off the edge from about an inch back of the point.
They don't need to shift the grip then because all they had
was a small sharp sliver of steel an inch long. They really
never wanted to kill anyone, especially by accident. They
just wanted to "cut 'em up a little." (I had some really nice
people for friends when I was young.)

I've saved the most practical and worthwhile method for
last. You simply hold it with one hand and open it with the
other. And you don't make any mistakes.

KNIFE LENGTH

Now let's talk about knife length.

Most states and cities have ordinances regarding the blade
length of knives. Length regulations vary from place to
place, often within the same state. Even the way the blade
length is measured varies. In some places, it's measured by
cutting edge alone, while in others, it's measured from the
pivot point of the knife.

Generally, it's considered illegal to carry any blade designed
for offense or defense. I don't know all the laws, not even in
the city and state where I live, so I'm not going to give any
legal advice at all. What I will talk about is the comparative
effectiveness of blade lengths.

There's a popular expression you can run across in many books: "The longer the knife, the bigger the punk!" Well, buddy, don't you believe it. The longer the knife, the more dangerous it is to face. It's not difficult to understand this, either. If their knife is longer than yours, they can cut you before you can cut them. A six-inch blade is vastly superior to one that is three inches long. But a six-inch blade is hurting when it's up against one that's eight inches long.

Having said that, I here have to say that the whole question of length is pretty nebulous. Somewhere in that range, length becomes less and less critical. It's largely a matter of taste. It depends on where you carry the knife, whether it's a folder or a fixed blade, and even how big you are. After all, a big man can more easily conceal a big knife.

What you have to keep in mind is the fact that a longer blade is just plain tough to go up against. This doesn't mean you're going to lose if the guy has a five-inch knife and yours is only three inches. It does mean you have to work harder to keep from getting hurt.

OTHER STREET WEAPONS

Knives aren't the only things used as street weapons. Man is a pretty inventive animal, and if there's one field where he really excels, it's in the field of weaponry. Baseball bats, chains, sticks, bricks—all of these have been used, and it's wise to remember them in case the need arises.

Although they are not really effective compared to a good knife, razors and ice picks are fairly popular, and they pack a lot of scare value into a relatively small amount of metal. Surprisingly, one of the most primitive weapons is also one of the best: a good solid hickory stick. It takes a lot of practice to overcome the tendency to merely use it as a club to hit with, but a good man with a stick is someone to be left strictly alone.

One of the most unusual and surprisingly effective weapons is a rolled-up magazine (*Life* had an ideal size and quality of paper for this). Roll the magazine very tightly and then use it as a thrusting stick. It's amazing how much damage can be done with such a weapon, especially when thrusts are directed at the nose, teeth, throat, solar plexus, and groin. You can roll it around the left arm and tape it in place, making

Many things can be used as street weapons. It's amazing how much damage can be done with a rolled-up magazine.

A magazine rolled around and taped to the left arm can make an effective shield.

an effective shield against both blows and cuts. Worn that way it could give real authority to an elbow smash.

I've seen some odd things used, but one of the oddest and dumbest I saw was when I was around nineteen. I knew a boy who was really hot after a couple of guys he felt had really done him wrong. He took an Irish potato, pressed a bunch of single-edged razor blades in it, edge out, then dropped it into a sock. He ran into the guys at a drive in, jumped out of his car cussing and swinging that sock. Everybody scattered because he was really swinging wild. He hit one guy on the shoulder, making some really nasty cuts. But then when he drew back, the sock bounced around and hit him in the back of the head. He yelped, jerked back and it bounced again and hit his hand. This time he dropped it and the other two closed in and damned near beat him to death.

I didn't know any of the people involved personally. They were just faces I saw around. I heard someone went to jail, but I'm not sure who.

Now the sock and razor blades is a real nice idea, but any fool can see that you have to tie it to the end of a stick to keep it from turning on you. And you damned well better practice with it before you go using it for real.

This is not a book about unconventional and makeshift weapons, so I won't be going into much detail about these things. But remember this: Almost anything can be used as a weapon when the need arises. What you have to do is look quickly and almost instantly evaluate the potential as a weapon of any object within reach. Flashlights and bottles are obvious, and a pencil or ball point pen makes a crude but effective stabbing instrument. A rock is not merely to throw, but can be used effectively as a hand ax. If you don't have anything, grab something, even if it's just your mother-in-law.

4

KNIFE CONCEALMENT

Concealing a knife and yet having it readily accessible is virtually an art form. It also requires a skill closely approaching that of a good stage conjurer. You must be able to move deftly and swiftly, and your audience needs to be just the tiniest bit distracted—at exactly the proper moment. I've known people who were simply incredible at getting a hidden knife out where it could be useful. With a bit of boastful modesty, let me say I wasn't too bad myself.

Back in my wild and rambunctious days, I carried a knife in my back pocket. I would make a couple of stitches in my pants so the knife would stand upright next to my wallet. This allowed me to hook my thumbs in my back pocket in a casual manner. I could walk around or merely hang about. In any sort of confrontation, this is not only a confident and aggressive posture, but a reassuringly normal one. But it also kept the knife well within reach if it were needed.

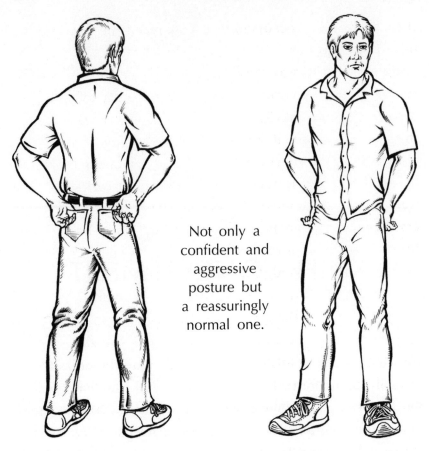

Not only a confident and aggressive posture but a reassuringly normal one.

This is so natural a stance that most people don't realize that your hands are hidden.

We had a saying about that: "When some clown hides his hands, hit 'em. You know he ain't gonna surprise you with a lollipop." Remember that. It was true then and it's true now.

The front pants pocket is also a good place to carry a knife, but it also requires the pants to be stitched. Done properly, the knife will ride flat against the leg and slightly below the top of the pocket. This way, you can carry change and keys and the knife, and they won't interfere with each other. The knife can be gotten pretty quickly by reaching in and gripping the blade with finger and thumb and popping it open.

There are all sorts of ways to hide a knife and I don't claim to know them all. At one time, I thought I did and then an incident occurred that convinced me I was still a babe in the woods.

About 1963, I was running a bar located in one of the rougher ghetto sections of Atlanta. I'd gotten to know the regulars and was having a pretty good time. I wasn't making any money but it was damn sure exciting.

One Saturday afternoon a very loud argument broke out between two of the regulars. It was getting serious, which was unusual since most of my trouble was caused by strangers. Regular customers don't want trouble in a bar because this causes the Man to show up and everyone had problems then. (I wholeheartedly agreed with this.)

I wandered down to that end of the bar and then really started to worry. The guy who was hot was a fellow named Zack, about forty-five and normally very quiet. Zack leaned on the bar, but Shorty, the other fellow, kept on yapping at him. I remember it very clearly. I was worried about a cutting and was watching to see if I could forestall trouble.

Zack turned and raised his hands high in the air, with the fingers of each hand spread. He wore a short sleeve shirt and the sleeves fell back to reveal bare, brown, and muscular arms.

"Shorty, you leave me the goddamn hell alone. Get that!" With each word he would jerk his arms to give them emphasis. When he finished his statement he turned back to the bar, folded his arms, and opened his knife.

I laid my hands on his arms and told him to cool it or he'd have the Man down all over me. I ran Shorty off and got everything calmed down.

And then I started to wonder, and I've wondered ever since. Where in the hell did that knife come from?

Standing where I was, I would have bet $100 that Zack had not gone for a knife, and I would have continued taking bets right up until I saw him open that knife. Standing where Shorty was, I would have bet $1,000 that Zack had no knife or any other kind of weapon. His arms were bare, ruling out an arm sheath. His hands never went close to his sides: they merely came down on the bar. He did not have the knife palmed: I could see the back of his hands and Shorty could see the front. But the knife opened up like magic.

My best guess so far is that he wore it under his collar. He could slip it out as his arms came down to the bar. But I really don't know. Wherever it was, I've never seen anything else quite so slick in all my born days.

I really wanted to ask him where he carried that knife, but just couldn't do that. Every social level has its own rules of etiquette. I was well liked and I wasn't about to sacrifice that goodwill by committing the gaucherie of inquiring about his knife. But I really wish I knew.

The main point to consider in concealing a knife is that it must be readily available. You can't really hide one from a thorough search, but that's not the purpose. The purpose is to keep it from being obvious that you're armed. Whether you do this from desire to catch someone off guard or to keep other folk from being disturbed by the realization you are armed is immaterial.

Above all, however, it must be available, and you must be practiced enough to get to it quickly.

Telling about where people conceal knives is not to suggest that you do the same. But it will make you aware of the places that are available, and it will also alert you to what some other guy might be doing.

Arm and shoulder sheaths are pretty good, but they generally require a coat or long-sleeved shirt. The exception is a sheath high on the upper arm that can be worn with short sleeves. It's secured by flat elastic and the knife is worn on the inside of the arm. It works pretty well.

Hats are also a good place to carry a knife. I had a buddy who used to wear an old slouch hat all the time. He carried his knife inside it, and if trouble seemed to be brewing, he would simply get nervous and take off his hat.

The smaller the knife, the easier it is to conceal. That's obvious. But don't assume a large knife can't be concealed. I used to wear a full-sized fighting knife with a nine-inch blade in a sheath I had made of very stiff leather. I could conceal it merely by wearing it upside down on my side. A coat hid it perfectly, and yet the knife was available almost instantly. The blade lay flat against the body and all that was necessary was to pop the snap and the blade was in the hand.

It's just human nature to jump at any good idea when you're trying to invent something like a place to conceal a knife. But always think your idea through to make sure it's practical. People have carried knives or guns concealed in a rolled-up newspaper or raincoat, for example, and I've always wondered about that. Sure, it conceals the knife, but who wants to walk around with something like that all the time? And what happens when you visit a bar? Are you going to maintain a death grip on your rolled-up newspaper all the time you're there? Why not just carry a sign saying that you've got a weapon concealed. Some people may be stupid, but there are a lot of them who aren't. Since you can handle the stupid people more easily than the smart ones, generally, for the sake of safety, always assume the one you'll run into is smart.

Let me end this with one more example before moving on to the more esoteric and erudite subjects. Several years ago, I had occasion to visit a large hospital in Atlanta to discuss with one of their doctors a lawsuit my company was involved in. I was waiting around outside the Outpatient Room where an old woman, as drunk as a skunk, was wandering around, talking to herself and picking up cigarette butts off the floor. Two young girls, both well dressed and attractive, started trying to take care of her. Evidently they did not know her but felt embarrassed by her behavior.

One finally got her to sit down and then patted her on the shoulder. She drew back, then patted her again.

"Honey, what's that?" she said, pointing to a barely noticeable lump under her sweater.

The woman glanced at her with a rather pitying expression on her face and moved with a speed no one would expect from a drunken old woman, whipping out a butcher knife with an eight-inch blade.

"Just my knife, child."

In my mind's eye, I pictured some young punk snatching *her* purse. Bet she could ruin his whole day.

5

WOUNDS

This section deals more with larger fighting knives than with the small folder or dagger. Larger knives deal more severe wounds, thus the fight is apt to be terminated more quickly. Nevertheless, I feel the information you're about to read is important and should be included in any book dealing with edged-weapon combat systems.

The controversy over point versus edge has raged for years. It was very much a major issue in the British military regarding the shape and use of the cavalry saber. The last issue saber [1912] was a pure thrusting weapon, so it might appear they had decided the thrust was superior to the cut, but that isn't quite true. At the time that saber was issued, there were many predicting all manner of dire consequences for a cavalry sword that relied on the use of the thrust only. And there were dire consequences, but they arose from the meeting of the cavalry with machine-gun fire. Those were dire consequences all right, but even a slashing sword wouldn't have helped and there was no point to further experiments with the design of the saber.

There was another fact that played an important role in the argument, however. The British always used steel scabbards for their swords. The slashing swords rarely had a sharp edge. Consequently, the damage inflicted was never as severe as it could have been. Steel scabbards are just not conducive to helping a sword maintain any sort of edge.

The British, however, encountered sharp slashing weapons on occasion and the damage was awesome. This was particularly true in India, where the results were far more lopped-off arms and legs than the British were prepared for.

Granted, there is a big difference between a cavalry saber and a three- or four-inch knife, but the lesson here is that all edges work better when they are sharp.

Medically speaking, a puncture wound is always considered more dangerous than a cut or open wound. The reason is that in a puncture, the damage cannot be examined easily, while with a cut or open wound the damage is easily visible. But a doctor isn't interested in inflicting damage. He wants to cure it. There's a big difference.

There's an old adage attributed to the Romans, who relied mainly on the thrust: "Two inches of steel in the right place will kill any man." It's pretty much true, but it does have a built-in fallacy: "... in the right place." Stabs in the throat, eye, heart, solar plexus, and a few other such places are frequently fatal and very quickly so. But the human body is large and these spots are small. What happens when you miss?

Many years ago, I was at a local bar with a close friend. I was paying the tab and my friend went on outside. I heard a lot of yelling and cursing and ran out to see what was happening. My friend was getting up off the ground and he still had a knife sticking in his stomach. Two brothers with whom he had been feuding had jumped him and stabbed him three times in the stomach. I got him to the hospital, and the doctors sewed him up. When the cops came, we told them we didn't know who the guys were and then left. Don had six stitches, two in each wound. The cops kept the knife, one of the Italian stilettos, but we didn't want it anyway. It seems the blade was dull and when it entered, it had merely pushed aside the entrails and whatever other organs it encountered. All my friend had was three small punctures of the skin and muscle. No big deal.

During the reign of Henri IV of France, a well-recorded duel occurred between the Sire La Garde and Sire Bazanez. As was the custom, the two principals met accompanied by their seconds. After the usual formalities, the four went at it, the principals engaging one another and the seconds doing the same. La Garde seems to have been the superior swordsman, as he soon landed a thrust on the forehead of Bazanez. The blade failed to penetrate the skull and the fight continued. La Garde then landed a thrust through the body and shortly thereafter, another. There was a momentary break and, when the action resumed, again La Garde sent the point of his sword through Bazanez's body.

At this point, Bazanez threw away his own sword and drew his dagger. "Look to it as you are a dead man!" he shouted and, dodging yet another thrust, leapt on his enemy. He stabbed him fourteen times in the neck and body. La Garde, while dying, managed to bite off half of Bazanez's chin.

Meanwhile, the seconds were finishing off their play. Mirabel, the brother of La Garde, landed a thrust through the body of Fermontez, the cousin of Bazanez. Fermontez managed to close with Mirabel, but was held and stabbed again, and so died. Mirabel offered to continue the fight with Bazanez, who declined on the grounds that he really needed to see a doctor, and rides away.

It would seem that not once did a stab land in the right place.

What all of this boils down to is that I feel the edge is superior in its ability to simply stop a fight and I think historical records lend credence to the idea. Consider the fact that most spears, at least those intended to be held in the hands, rather than thrown, have provisions to keep an opponent from running up the blade and shaft. A thrust in the body may kill your opponent, but that doesn't help you if he lives long enough to see you dead.

The thrust or stab is risky because it can kill and yet not stop. In most street encounters, killing is not desired, but stopping is. The cut will stop but not kill.

Now, having said the edge is better than the point, let me bring up a very important consideration. Trying to predict how a man will react when injured is impossible. Some will fall down screaming from a very minor wound, while others will keep on coming despite the most awful and awesome of injuries. There is simply no way to tell beforehand how a specific person will behave.

Any encounter involving a knife is serious. It's no game. A game has a set of rules and a goal, which remain invariable. But an encounter with a knife, indeed any life-and-death combat situation, will be governed by the circumstances and the goals of the participants.

Consider, for example, the commando raid where the killing of a sentry and doing it quietly are the prime goals. Compare this with a street encounter with a young tough out to impress himself and cut you up. What do you do?*

Finally, in the hopes of nailing the point home, consider the well-known Colonel Jim Bowie. During the fight at the Vidalia Sand Bar, he received two gunshots wounds and a thrust through the chest with a sword cane. He still killed his man.

---

* Editor's note: page 23 of original manuscript missing here.

6

USING THE KNIFE

We've all seen the Hollywood knife fight: two men, facing each other with blades bared, circling, arms outstretched. Someone slashes and his opponent dodges. Then another slash, blocked by the other knife. Then suddenly the two close, each grabbing the other's knife hand. Muscles straining, arm to arm, locked into an embrace of death!

Whee! Romantic and inspiring. And pure and utter garbage.

In real life, a knife encounter is usually too fast for the eye to follow. Two guys will be arguing, getting hotter and hotter. One suddenly appears to back down, usually saying something like, "I don't want no trouble." He turns his back, then spins back around. There's a brief flash and the other guy is lying on the ground, bleeding and screaming. If he's real brave, he's only moaning a little.

If you are ever so unlucky as to get close to a real knife fight, it would be useful to keep one fact in mind above all others: the real knife fighter does not wish to engage in a fight.

He doesn't care who is best with a knife. He only wants to cut you. He will then do anything he can to take you by surprise, attack, and finish you off before you can fight back.

In those cases where both parties manage to get their knives out, one of two things has happened: one of the fighters is a complete turkey who gave his opponent a chance to fight back; or both fighters are pretty shrewd and not about to allow the other one any advantage that can be prevented.

A book I once read about gunfighters in the Old West had a quote that summed things up perfectly. When questioned about attitudes, an old man who had been there replied, "Well, it's like this. I don't like that sonofabitch, and I'm gonna kill him the first *good* chance I get."

Times have changed, of course. But people haven't.

It's difficult to write about the mental aspects of an armed encounter. I've met and discussed this with many men who have been in combat, from police shootouts to military action in Guadalcanal, Korea, and Vietnam. I grew up in an area where knifings were commonplace. I tended a bar in a neighborhood where killings were not uncommon. And I've had a few hairy encounters myself.

It's amazing how varied the attitudes of these people are. But there do seem to be connecting, underlying threads.

One is the acceptance of fear. Fear that makes you sweat and your heart beat like a trip-hammer. Fear can kill you, of course, but if you accept it, you can use it to speed up reaction time, gain alertness, and excuse some savagery you would normally not even consider.

The other element is the acceptance of pain, and the ability to subordinate pain to a larger, more important goal. I once talked to a Marine who had won the Congressional Medal of Honor in Korea. He lost a leg in the process. He confessed to me that the leg was shattered *before* the action started. He said that it hurt like hell, but he had no choice but to keep fighting because otherwise he'd be dead. He figured he could live without a leg...

Here's a bit of personal philosophy I developed pretty young in life. Over the years, I haven't changed it at all. I prefer to leave people alone. I won't bother them and all I ask is that they not bother me. There are a helluva lot of really tough people out there and if you bother them, they will hurt you. The pain and trouble really aren't worth it.

Now, if you've grasped, really grasped, what we've been talking about, I can go on to the technical fine points. If you haven't, I'd suggest you would have been smarter to buy more insurance than to buy this book.

It's relatively simple to grip a folding knife. You hold it blade out like a sword and edge down like an ax. With larger knives, there are questions about where to hold your thumb, but with a pocket knife, it's not a problem: you hold it the best way you can. Above all, you grip your knife tightly.

People who are lucky enough to have no experience of knives often think a blade merely slides in and out of a target, and that very little shock is transmitted to the hand. That's not so. Unless you maintain a tight grip at all times, you will learn one of the most unsettling lessons in combat—either a stab or a cut can tear the knife out of a hand that doesn't hold it tightly.

For some reason, a few instructors have decided the best way to hold a knife is in the "icepick" grip with the blade lying flat along the underside of the forearm. Now, think about this and you might decide it's really not smart. The first thing it costs you is reach. When you try to close in on an opponent, and you're holding your knife in that way and he isn't, he will probably cut you first. That's the second thing it costs you.

The more stubborn advocates of this method of holding the knife will argue that you can conceal the knife until the last

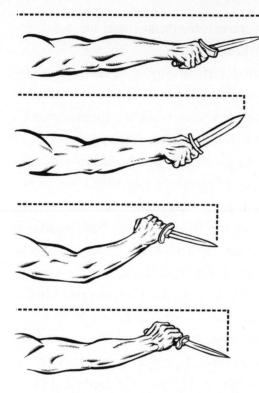

The icepick grip: the first thing it costs is reach.

minute with this grip. All I can say is that it might work if your opponent is carrying a tin cup and wears dark glasses. Otherwise, you're wishing for too much of a combination of stupidity and bad luck.

It's important to hold the knife with the edge down. How important? Well, it depends. How important is your life? Holding the blade with the edge up may look tough and macho, but looks are not what count here. Holding the blade up limits your maneuverability. It is much easier to turn the blade over and cut up than to turn it over so you can rip down.

A lot of paperback writers remark how their characters hold the blade edge up, like a well-trained knife-fighter, but authors don't have to worry about who their opponent is. Many of them don't even bother to pick up a knife and see how it feels. They simply copy what they've read by other incompetent writers.

Any serious social encounter with knives has one main goal: to stop the action. Beyond that, you have a little flexibility: to kill, or merely get away, or what have you. But first comes the cessation of hostilities.

There are many ways to handle this. You can run, shoot, call the cops, or even try to organize a discussion group to talk the problem out. But I'm talking knives, so I'll limit myself to that.

This brings us back to a previous subject: wounds. All wounds are painful and pain is a great tool for stopping fights. So is the loss of use of various parts of the body. Therefore, it follows that although we wish to inflict any wound we can, the more painful it is, the better.

A cut that lands on the lower forearm at right angles is painful and will inflict a certain amount of damage. But a right-angle cut will only go so deep before it encounters the bone. But if you change the angle, you can cut more flesh before you hit bone. If you hit it at the correct angle, the blade can skate along the bone, peeling a very large section of meat. I can assure you that people do not continue fighting with the flesh of the forearm peeled back from the wrist to the elbow.

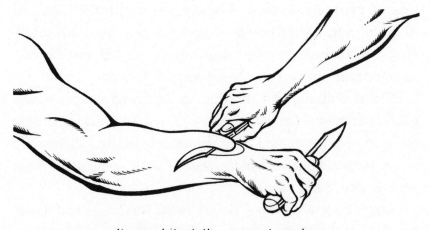

It you hit at the correct angle,
the blade can skate along the bone.

The same can be said for a cut to the ribs. Angle the cut and the blade cuts more flesh, therefore giving a great deal more pain. Loose flaps of skin are disconcerting to the man on whom they flap.

This principle works also with the stab. A straight in and out puncture inflicts damage, but if you go in at one angle and out at another, you do more damage. Obviously you don't want to hang around probing, since that gives him too much opportunity to cut you. But if you stab or thrust and, as you withdraw the blade, twist it, then lever up or down or sideways, you can do a lot more damage. And it doesn't take any additional time, it can all be done in one fluid motion.

I was at a bar one night when a fight broke out in the parking lot. Being, in those days, an always interested bystander, I wandered out to watch the action. The two guys had just started. One had managed to get his jacket wrapped around his left arm. The other guy had a very slight nick on his side and just a spot of blood. I suspected the first guy had tried to cut him, missed doing any damage, and backed off to slip off his jacket.

I knew both of them, although not well. They were considered pretty hard cases. Bobby, the one with the jacket on his arm, had a reputation of being a real top-flight SOB. He'd cut his brother pretty badly in an argument at home, so upsetting his parents they'd kicked him out.

He was bobbing and weaving while his opponent, whom I never knew by any name other than Junior, was standing more or less flat-footed, but always moving in. There were a few passes, none of which landed. Both combatants were serious and quiet.

I noticed a strange thing. Bobby's coat was looser and looser on his arm. Every time he moved the left arm, the coat was wrapped a little less tightly. I wondered if Junior noticed.

When Bobby made his move, I saw that Junior had.

Bobby's move was to fake a cut and snap the coat out at Junior's head, then move in with the knife. Junior was a real pro. He grabbed the coat and yanked. Bobby stumbled forward and got two quick swipes across his belly. He fell and started yelling to beat the band. Can't say I blame him, either.

(Sometimes, by the way, things just don't go right. Some girl told the cops who did it and Junior spent a year in jail.

Bobbing and weaving leads to a
fake to the head and a cut to the leg.

I never heard of him again. But Bobby spent three months in the hospital and six in jail. Later, he was shot to death robbing a liquor store.)

Looking back and evaluating it on the basis of skill, there were a lot of good moves. Bobby played it cool, protecting his left arm and also preparing to use his coat to distract his opponent. He made one mistake. He should have braced for a yank or else let go of the coat.

Junior, of course, played an even better game. He saw the coat being unwound (done very well, I should state), but never let on he was aware of it. He deliberately came in close enough that he could be hit with the coat and was ready to take care of the move.

The whole fight took maybe one and a half or two minutes. But it was quick. Both combatants were thinking fast and moving well. One just thought a little faster than the other.

And that's one of the keys: alertness. You have to be constantly alert. No one knows all the tricks; new ones are being thought of all the time. So expect to see something new and unexpected. If you're alert, you can avoid being killed by it.

That brings us to the subject of distractions. You can't afford to be distracted. At the same time, you have to be aware of everything that goes on. It's very much like a juggling act in your mind.

At the same time you have to avoid distractions, you should be searching for some way to distract your opponent. Junior distracted Bobby by letting him think his trick with the coat was going to work. If you can get an opponent's attention on the wrong thing for just a moment, you have sufficient time to move in and back out.

You must also remember the street is filled with weapons. There are common ones that everyone knows: sticks, bottles, rocks. But there are others that most people don't think about. Take a bright light from a street light—if you can maneuver so that it's in his eyes (and, incidentally, keep him from maneuvering so it's in your eyes). A tree stump, the curb, or uneven pavement offer the opportunity to make your opponent stumble, if you can take advantage of it. Looked at from that point of view, you can make the whole area in which the fight takes place into a weapon.

It's more common to think of these elements as "tactical terrain advantage," but I think you gain a psychological advantage by simply regarding them as a weapon. The term "weapon" has a less pedantic ring than "tactical terrain advantage," and it's nicely suggestive. Remember: your frame of mind is always your chief weapon.

Stance is also important because, from there, you will move into your attacks as well as your defense. It should be remembered that when you're out of range, your stance doesn't matter. Hell, you can hold your knife in your teeth, if your opponent can't reach you with his. Just be able to get the damned thing back in your hand when he starts to close in on you.

With large knives, a lot of people advocate a modified fencing stance. The theory here seems to be that since swords and knives are both edged weapons, why then, sauce for the goose tastes just as good on a gander. Well, I can tell you a goose can have a gamier taste and require a more pungent sauce.

The difference between swords and knives is this: a sword is both an offensive and defensive weapon, whereas a knife is not. The attack is delivered with the sword and it is defended against by the sword.

But a knife, regardless of size, is an offensive weapon. It has defensive capabilities, but they are highly limited and, because of length, do not include the practical capability of blocking another knife.

Let me illustrate this with an experiment. Roll up two sections of newspaper. Have a friend take one of them and use it as if he were cutting and thrusting, while you try to block with the other. As long as he makes straightforward moves, you'll be all right; in fact, if you're an experienced fencer, you may find yourself doing quite well.

But the moment your opponent starts to fake and cut, or merely attack and let the blade drop or rise high, you're lost. The two blades are simply too short to guarantee you'll be able to make contact consistently enough to parry or block.

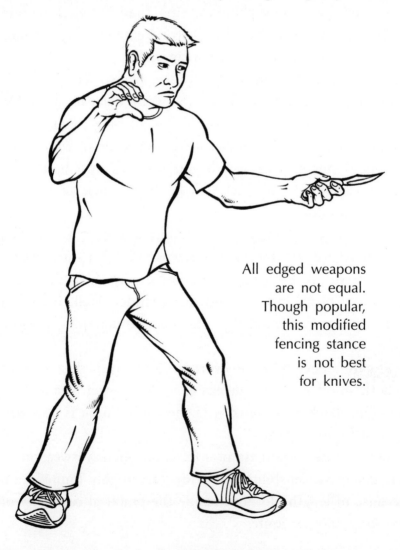

All edged weapons are not equal. Though popular, this modified fencing stance is not best for knives.

The stance that gives the best protection while offering the greatest latitude in your attack is a modified boxing stance—that, of a left hand boxer with a right hand lead.

Right leg and arm are slightly forward. The body is in a slight crouch. The left arm is back, and I would suggest you keep your left hand closed tightly in a fist. It's threatening, can be used to punch with, and the fist can give speed and authority to a blocking movement.

Keep both arms close to the body, elbows in. Stand face on to your opponent. This offers pretty good protection for the vital areas. Arms protect the sides, the forearms and hands guard the face, and the elbows give a reasonable amount of protection to the midsection and chest.

From this position, you can also launch an attack in almost any direction. You can slash from either side, give a full fencer's lunge, and even switch hands quickly and easily.

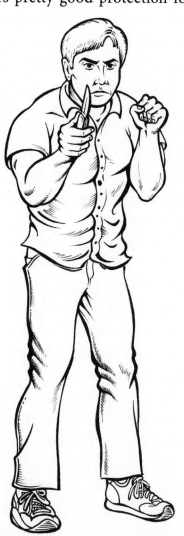

A modified boxing stance gives better protection plus offers leeway for different attacks.

It's useful to teach yourself to switch the knife from one hand to the other. It can allow you to attack quickly from a totally unexpected quarter and it can let you set up distracting movements. If you switch hands and attack, and don't finish the fight, you can fake a hand switch and attack with the primary. But switching hands is tricky and there are a lot of opportunities to screw up attempting it.

Once more, I can best show you what I mean by going back nostalgically to those glorious misspent days of my youth. I'm thinking particularly of one summer night in the park when I and my friends were engaged in our usual occupations of girl-watching and wise-assing. A commotion started suddenly at the entrance to the pavilion and sorta flowed in—like water into a gutter.

Someone none of us knew had made an entrance and was doing his best to give the impression he was as bad as they come. He walked straight down the path, not moving aside for anyone or anything. He bumped men, women, little kids, and girls. The whole world just had to know how tough he was.

There was a guy in the park we called "Smokey Stover" after a comic strip character. He was a few years older than my friends and me, and he was mean all the way through. Well, Tall Tough Stranger bumped right into Smokey. Smokey never batted an eye, just slapped the boy with his open hand.

Tall Tough Stranger jumps back and starts talking the Bad Talk, fumbles in his pocket and, with a very loud click, pops open one of those damn Italian switchblades. Smokey just stood there. He'd already thumbed his knife open and had it dangling at his side.

It's a good bet TTS had seen *Rebel Without a Cause*, because as he advanced in a low crouch, arms real wide, he tossed his knife from hand to hand. I don't mean he switched his knife from hand to hand. I mean he *tossed* it so that it traveled a couple of feet through the air. He was good. He must have spent hours in front of the mirror, practicing the trick. Too bad he didn't take fifteen minutes thinking about it.

Smokey leaped forward and he looked like he belonged in a movie himself. It was a beautiful, long, low lunge worthy of Errol Flynn or Stewart Granger. He was tall and skinny with a lot of reach anyway. His knife was aimed right at the eye of TTS. TTS made a beautiful leap straight back.

The problem was, he was right in the middle of one of those impressively practiced knife tosses of his. When he jumped back to avoid the point of Smokey's weapon, he left his hanging in midair.

Smokey kicked the knife away and TTS looked upset at that. It was nothing, however, compared with how upset he was about to look. I guess he had reason.

Looking back, the whole thing seems damned stupid for

Rebel without
a chance.

the simple reason that it was. First of all, no one went looking for a fight in the park. They happened there all the time,
but the object was to avoid them without being stepped on.
King Kong walked softly there. So TTS wasn't real bright
to push into things there to begin with.

Secondly, he didn't seem to understand that knives are
real. They make real cuts and the blood you bleed is real,
and the pain is damned real.

And last, why hadn't he realized that switching a knife
from hand to hand is one thing—but sacrificing control of
your weapon is something else altogether.

He also forgot—or never figured out—the cardinal rule of
survival. Always remember: you never know who the other
guy is until you fight him. And by that time it might be
too late to do anything about it.

Smokey Stover was the stuff of legends in our little circle.
Everyone knew he carried a knife and would rather cut you
than eat. I never heard of him being in a fistfight. If you got
into a fight with him you had to cut him first, or maybe hit
him with a baseball bat. Otherwise you'd get cut.

PRIMARY TARGETS

When forced into a position of having to use a knife against
a similarly armed opponent, your primary targets should be
the knife hand and arm. Of the two, the arm is the better
target. It is larger, providing more area to cut, and damage
there can affect the ability of your opponent to hold his
knife. Don't pass up the hand, but try for the arm.

Most knife fighters will assume a stance that protects the
body, neck, and face by covering them with the arms and
moving them slightly out of your range. If you can land a
blow to the head, by all means do so, especially if the blood

When facing another knife-wielder, go for the knife hand and arm.

will run into your opponent's eyes. Scalp wounds bleed copiously, far in excess of the actual damage done, and it's hard to fight when a heavy stream of your own blood is obstructing your vision.

Either hand is a good target. With a big knife, you can go so far as to lop off fingers given the opportunity. But a small knife can still cut deeply, especially if you remember to angle the cut. A few such wounds and just about anyone will be ready to call it a day.

In any one-on-one situation, remember the words of George Silver: "That there be no wards or grips, and to use continual motion."

There are no specific parries that can be made in a knife fight because there are no specific cuts or stabs to watch for. Since the knife hand and arm are targets, it follows that they should be moving because a moving target is harder to hit. Bobbing and weaving the whole body might help a little, but above all it is the arms that should be moving when you are in range of your opponent's knife. When out of range, it doesn't matter. You can rest, so long as you don't go to sleep. But once you're in range of his knife, you have to keep moving.

The ability to judge distance accurately is critical. When your opponent attacks, you have to be able to tell if his knife will land or fall short a few inches. If he lunges, will his blade reach you? In an actual battle, you'll find yourself constantly assessing such things.

The idea is to stay out of range until you are ready to attack, or receive his attack and counter. Counter-cutting can be very deadly. If an attack is made and fails to hit the mark, the attacker has put himself in his opponent's reach

Staying out of range.

A counter-cut when opponent is within reach

and is vulnerable until he pulls back. If the opponent moves at the right moment, and with a good counter, the fight is over then and there.

There are tricks you can employ to confuse your opponent's ability to judge distance. One is to hold the knife very close to the blade. If you can safely do so, make a couple

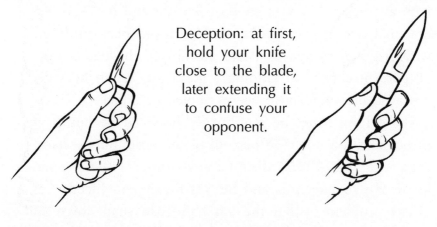

Deception: at first, hold your knife close to the blade, later extending it to confuse your opponent.

Old fencing trick.

of passes that fall short. (Your opponent will probably assist you here.) Then shift the knife forward until it's extended as much as possible, and attack. This will add to your reach and his consternation...

There's an old fencing trick that can be adapted here, as well. Since the lunge is made from the left foot, draw the left foot close to the right. Your opponent will judge your effective distance from your normal position, but when you lunge forward, your reach will be greater than he expects.

I once taught a judo and self-defense class at a YMCA that had a fencing team. One of the fencers was interested in knives, so we made some dummy knives to work out with after class. He was good at fencing and had won several matches in the Southeast. He moved beautifully and with frightening speed. When he lunged, he had about a 30 percent chance of landing a good hit. When he failed, however, he would have been crippled or killed.

For a long time, he stubbornly believed he could get through with a lunge 90 percent of the time. But he hadn't seen what I had, and didn't know some of the people I knew. We kept records and he was finally convinced.

The problem is that the left hand can snap down and

block a lunge, leaving you completely open to a counter. Or else the right hand, holding the knife, can drive the point into your arm, causing you to slice your own forearm as you move forward.

Fencing lunges are always preceded by some fake or series of attacks designed to bring the opposing sword out of line so that the thrust can reach home. This isn't possible with a knife, so the thrust and lunge have to be made as a single movement, with speed as the keynote for success. It just doesn't work all the time.

To sum all this up, I would advise you against lunging. You're safer staying with cuts to the arm and leg until you can move in and finish your opponent off safely.

Left hand snaps down and blocks your lunge,
leaving you open to a counter.

Feints are the order of the day. If you can make an opponent think you're attacking in one area while your real goal is elsewhere, you can land; and that's what you want to do. A fake cut at the head, followed by a drop down to the leg for a slice, sounds difficult and time consuming, but you'd be surprised how quick it is and how well it can work.

There's no way I can list all the possible feints that can be used in knife fighting. To list those I know about would be simply to not list those I haven't thought of. The most important skill in combat is the ability to think and there is no better way to practice that than to try developing your own feints.

Parries usually require the left arm, but you need to learn to use both arms in blocking. Not everyone is right handed and the lefty with any experience at all will have the advantage of being used to facing right-handed people. But never forget, if you're right handed and find yourself facing a left-handed opponent, that if switching hands works for you, it can also work for him. A good trick is to keep the left hand clenched into a fist, as this really adds a positive force to a block and also keeps your fingers out of the way of the knife. It's rather disconcerting to suddenly lose a finger.

I've not said much about punches, not because I intend to ignore them, but because I don't want to make a big issue out of throwing one. If you can hook or jab, do so. Just remember he has a knife. A block can get you cut at the same time.

Back when I was young, in the days before the advent of karate, you could kick a man rather easily. Most people simply did not expect a kick. They were too used to fists to think about feet. Alas, such is not the case anymore. Nowadays people expect kicks.

High kicks are generally worthless. To start with, it takes a lot of practice to learn how to get one to land properly. Even then they are just too slow. They are also easy to block, and when blocked, leave the kicker in a dangerous position.

Now, you may disagree with that statement, particularly if you've had some martial arts training. I suggest you look at a full contact karate match some time. The rules require

One of many possible feints:
a fake cut at the head, followed by
a drop down to the leg for a slice.

contestants to deliver so many kicks per round. What generally happens is that the opponents run out, give the required number of kicks, and then proceed to beat the hell out of each other.

Low kicks can be useful. You can deliver one quickly and with devastating force. A kick to the knee is especially painful, and if done right, can cripple someone for life. The groin, although easier to protect by shifting the body, is also a fine fight-stopping target.

A fake attack followed by a kick and then a real attack is a generally reliable strategy. You can modify it to a fake kick and a real attack, or to any combination you like. But remember: *a good, low kick, not going any higher than the groin* is an effective weapon.

Throwing things—dust, rocks, change, just anything—at your opponent is a time-honored gimmick and, as gimmicks go, okay. But it's overrated and very familiar. A good, cool fighter can slide aside, duck, and recover to meet your attack. And if your opponent is wearing glasses, well, what's the point of throwing dirt in his face?

Pepper was supposed to be popular at one time and when I roamed the streets, I heard about people carrying it, but I never saw anyone use it. The trouble with gimmicks like that is that everyone had heard about them and it's hard to surprise someone with something he knows about.

Of course, what goes for rocks and pepper goes for the trick of flicking a cigarette in a man's face. But there is a little-known gimmick that can be added to that one: wetting the end of the cigarette before you flick it. If the wet end hits, it has a tendency to stick for a moment, which can hurt and be distracting.

If you want to throw something, look for a brick. Better yet, look for half a brick. Grab it, get in close, and smash.

✧   ✧   ✧

So far, we've discussed fights where the knives are of relatively equal length. But what can you do when you have only your three-and-a-half-inch blade and your opponent pulls one that's eight to twelve inches long?

To put it bluntly, you have a real problem in that case.

Against a longer knife, you can't really go for hand cuts. It's just too easy for him to cut you before you even reach his hand or arm. This is just as true for attacks to the body. By the time your blade has reached his chest (assuming you're both pretty much the same height), his blade has already gone into you five to nine inches.

One of my cardinal rules in knife fighting is to avoid getting cut, and I advise you to do the same. But if you find yourself unable to escape a situation like this, there are some things you can try. I wish I could tell you they work all the time, but they don't. If you do well the maneuver I'm about to describe, you probably have a 40 percent chance of success. If you do it very well, you can even your chances.

First, let me elaborate a little on hand cuts. When you're fighting with a knife the same size as your opponent's, you can attack at the hand from a high position, cutting downward then dropping the wrist and flicking the knife around so that you actually cut from the inside. But when your opponent has a longer knife, he can always stay out of your range while working on your hands. As I said, you have a problem.

Virtually the only way to deal with the situation is to reverse your stance, with your left foot forward. The rule is to protect your knife hand. You may have to take some cuts on the left arm, but the fighting arm has to be protected.

As your opponent attacks, attempt to fend him off with the left hand and counter-cut with your knife. *This is a high risk maneuver*, but if it works, you can make your move. Nothing tricky, nothing special, no big secret. You just leap forward, trying to close with him as quickly as you can. If you can land on one of his feet, so much the better. Not to break his instep, but to throw him off balance and prevent retreat. As you close, cut and stab in a frenzy of motion. You have only a fraction of a second before he will bring his knife into play. During that time, you have to hit something vital or incapacitating—throat, eyes, solar plexus, groin—and the

Attack at the hand from a high position,
cutting downward, then dropping the wrist and
flicking the knife around to cut from the inside.

attacks must be vicious. Twist and rip for all you're worth. If you fail, you will never have a second chance.

Should the situation be reversed and your opponent have the shorter knife, remember the above. He has to close with you in order to make his weapon effective. Don't allow yourself to be worked into a corner where you can't retreat. Move away, move in to attack, then move back out again. Take full advantage of your longer reach.

When you have the shorter knife,
reverse your stance to protect your knife hand,
then move in close and attack quickly,
aiming to incapacitate.

Should he manage to close in, however, you have to retaliate in kind, stabbing and cutting in a frenzy of motion at least the equal of his.

FIGHTING TWO AT ONCE

If fighting a man with a longer knife is bad, fighting two men is even worse. If they know what they're doing, they'll cut you to ribbons. The only hope you have is the fact that very few people work well as a team.

Back in the mid-1970s, when I lived in Birmingham, Alabama, a good friend of mine found himself in this position when two guys tried to roll him. He's a relatively mild sort, but he had the benefit of a misspent youth and was pretty streetwise. What happened is a rather classic approach and not a bad way to handle it.

The two men approached and one walked directly in front of him while the other walked to the side, eyes straight ahead.

As soon as the second was behind my friend, the first snarled a few curses, put his hand in his pocket and demanded money. My friend, being a very reasonable man, reacted in a reasonable way. He spun, lashed out with a low kick that caught the guy in back of him square in the crotch, continued the spin and popped the other guy on the nose with his fist. He then moved back, thumbed open his knife and started forward. His bad knee gave way, so he stumbled, which gave the two time to hobble away, clutching various parts of their wounded anatomy. Had the leg not given way, I'm sure he would have been in some serious trouble for cutting up some people, but then again, maybe not. I don't think he really cared.

The point is, he reacted in a totally unexpected way. He attacked. He did it quickly, viciously, and with dedication to wreaking harm on his attackers. He then backed off, armed himself, and was about to renew the battle.

When faced with two men with knives, this is by far your best defense. Attack one, then turn the fake into a real attack on the other. Whether the attack succeeds or not, you should be able to split the two apart and that should give you time to run. If the attack works and you can disable one, then it's the old one-on-one. Otherwise, just run. Two men are just too many for one guy to face.

FIGHTING WHEN UNARMED

Equally frightening is to be attacked by one man who has a knife when you're unarmed.

A lot of books on self-defense describe neat disarming moves, and if you believe them, you must think it's the easiest thing in the world to subdue a man with a knife. Ha.

Of course, it's possible to disarm a knife wielder. If he's not familiar with knives or if he's afraid of it, it's quite possible. If, on the other and more likely hand, he knows what he's doing, you have almost no chance at all.

Earlier I stated that the practiced knife fighter is not interested in seeing who is the best man, but only in cutting you. It doesn't matter if you're unarmed or not.

I never met anyone who was good with a knife who did not regard each and every adversary with a great deal of fear and respect. No matter who he fought, he regarded that opponent as the toughest and most deadly person he was ever likely to meet. Any and all attacks would be made with a great deal of caution and restraint. He would always be alert for any trick that might be attempted.

Facing a man who regards you as a totally unknown danger and threat to his existence doesn't leave you much room. He isn't about to extend himself in a wild lunge so that you can grab his knife arm, yank forward, and smash your hand against his elbow. He won't attack you with an overhand stab so you can cross block and then slip into an armlock. He will attack you just as if you had a knife, too. Feints, hand cuts, moving in and out. Cutting and weakening you until he can move in and make a kill safely.

I can offer no ways that give you a relatively high chance of success when forced to face a knife unarmed. There are things you can try, but how well they work is problematic. But any attack is better than giving up and waiting like a sheep to die, standing around and bleating.

The eyes are a highly vulnerable and sensitive area. Any attack in this area is likely to produce a certain degree of panic, particularly if it is quick and vicious. This is a last-ditch, desperation move because the moment you initiate it you are completely vulnerable.

That said, the move itself is simple. You leap in, grab the head with your hands on either side and dig your thumbs in at the eyes. You'll probably get cut, but it only takes a second to dig in at the cornea and blind a man permanently. If I'm going to die, I'd like to at least leave my killer something to remember me by.

Wrist grabbing is a very chancy thing. Until a few years ago, I would have said it's impossible, but then something happened in a practice session that changed my mind. But I still wouldn't want to rely on it.

A close friend, John Roberts, was on his way to Vietnam and spent a few days with me. I questioned him about the hand-to-hand training he'd received as a Green Beret and one thing led to another, so we made up some practice knives and headed to the yard. I was doing rather well (John may try to bomb me if he reads this), when suddenly I slipped on the grass and fell. John, having all the honorable instincts of a rattlesnake, instantly jumped in and tried to do me in.

I was reacting with a mild case of panic and trying to ward off his attack with my left arm when suddenly I brushed his knife arm. My hand slid down his arm and I found myself gripping his wrist. Not one to pass up an advantage, I yanked and he fell forward onto my "knife."

So it's possible. But again, I have no wish to rely on it. However, if it does happen that you do manage to grab the knife arm, clutch the hand, not just the wrist. With only the wrist being held, the knife can be levered down and used to cut your hand. Or it can be switched to the other hand. The best place to grip the hand is just back of the guard. This gives you some leverage and—who knows?—it might even be possible to you to get it away from him.

Just grabbing the knife is no real solution to your problem. Obviously, you need to do something more—biting, kicking,

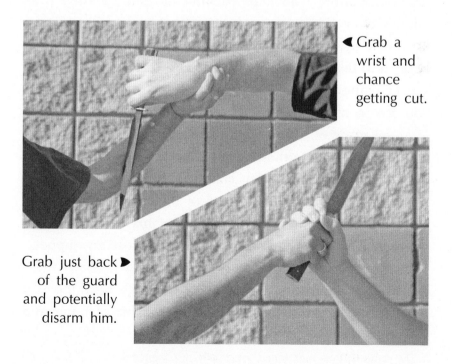

◀ Grab a wrist and chance getting cut.

Grab just back ▶ of the guard and potentially disarm him.

punching, anything. The body is full of vulnerable spots, so make the most of them.

This is no self-defense book, so I'm not going to talk about pressure points. A medical text on anatomy will tell you what you want to know if you take the time to study it. You do need to learn where they are, how to attack them, and what happens when you do.

But keep one important thing in mind if you ever face a knife attack while you're unarmed: you have almost no odds of surviving.

A friend of mine beat those odds, once, and beat them damned well. His name was Don* and he was about three years older than me. He was one of the toughest people I've ever run across. In Korea, he was highly decorated and badly wounded.

We had been to the local movie when the fight broke out. I ran to see what was happening and saw a guy try-ing to cut Don, who kept backing up and avoiding him. I knew Don didn't have a knife with him because I'd just borrowed it to open some boxes. I started to move in and help, but Don waved me back. The guy with the knife wasn't real good. He kept making the sort of wild slashes you see in movies.

As he made one, Don slipped to the side and lashed out with his foot, taking the boy's legs from under him. The kid hit the ground and Don was standing over him. He stomped him in the mouth with the heel of his boot and then piv-oted. The kid on the ground lost all of his front teeth and you could hear his jaw pop. I damn near lost my supper.

Don later confessed that he felt real lucky.

You can't count on luck, however. Quick thinking is a must. Quick thinking, combined with a bit of lying and

---

* The same Don as mentioned previously in Chapter 5.

deception is nothing short of deadly, especially when combined with experience.

I watched a fight that broke out one night between a couple of over-age high school students who didn't know each other. They exchanged a couple of punches. Then one broke away, ran to his car and grabbed a piece of pipe he had there. He started at the other, who backed off, looking for something.

Somebody in the crowd yelled, "Bust his goddamn head, Bobby."

The other boy stopped, held up his hand and said, "Whoa, wait a minute. What's your last name?"

The other glared and secured his grip on the pipe before answering, "Strickland. Bobby Strickland."

"Strickland! Bobby Strickland? Well, I'll be goddamned. Man, you're my cousin."

"Boy, you're crazy, you ain't no damn kin to me."

"Hell yes, I am. I'm your cousin. Hell, I ain't gonna fight my own cousin. My momma would tear me up if she found out. Hell, let's just call it quits."

With that, he simply walked forward with his right hand outstretched with an offer to shake. The other guy hesitated and that was all it took. The boy got closer, promptly kicked him where it hurt, thumbed his knife and slashed Bobby across the chest.

He ran like hell and everyone could hear him laughing.

Two of my favorite stories concern the same boy. Let's call him Harvey (his real name was just as bad). He was a really mean and nasty guy. He had quite a reputation as a street fighter and I believe it is probably well deserved. Harvey had never taken a bath in his life and you could smell him a mile away. Many a night I've been talking with some guys and someone would sniff and say, "Here comes Harvey," and sure enough, there he would be. He won his fights by getting in close. Sooner or later the other guy would have to breathe and when he did, he'd gag on the stench.

Harvey was pretty big, about six-foot-two and two hundred thirty-five pounds. He wore his hair in a crewcut about two inches long. It stood straight up.

He and some other boy got into it one night at a drive-in. I don't know who the other guy was, but Harvey wouldn't make a move. Finally the boy said, "Harvey, you're a goddamn coward. You wouldn't hit me with a stick."

"Yeah hell I would."

The boy walked over to a trash pile, picked up a two-by-four and walked over to Harvey. Proferring the stick, he said, "Here, goddamn it. Hit me with it."

Moving really well, Harvey snatched the stick and slammed it down on the fool's head. The boy fell like a poleaxed steer, blood gushing from his scalp.

Harvey looked down and said, "I told him I'd hit 'im with it."

The other story about Harvey also concerns Smokey Stover, whom we've met before. It happened at a drive-in movie. Smokey was an inch taller, but a good seventy-five pounds lighter. As should be expected, out popped the knife. Harvey wanted no part of that, but he didn't back down, either.

"Hey, man, I ain't got no knife. If I had a knife, I'd fight you but I ain't got one."

There was a crowd gathered and when he said that, at least twenty people held out knives, butt-first and yelled, "Here, take mine."

Harvey paid no attention. He didn't want to see them. He just kept backing up and saying that if he had a knife he'd fight.

Smokey was unimpressed. He just kept coming.

When Harvey made his move, it was as fast as I've ever

seen a man move. He just turned and ran. Just flat got it down the road.

You see, Harvey understood fighting.

Even so, Harvey's dead. Years after he ran from Smokey, he shot a man and got life in prison. While he was there, somebody chopped him with an ax. It was no real loss to the world.

So where does all this leave us?

Knife fighting is neither glamorous nor heroic. It is a quick and dirty affair that leaves everyone feeling soiled.

A man who deliberately tries to get into a knife fight is a damn fool. To risk your life, that of a stranger, and the well-being of friends and relatives for some childish, macho self-image is the height of stupidity.

However, it is equally stupid in this day and age to go around unprepared and denying such things happen. They happen, and I'm a firm believer in trying to make sure they don't happen to me.

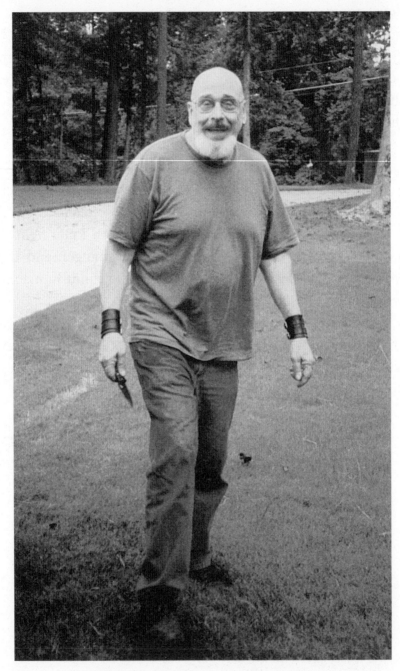

Photo of Hank taken by Greg Phillips.

HANK'S STUDENTS

Editor's Note: We asked Hank's pupils to contribute to this volume by talking about aspects of knives and knife fighting they had learned from Hank. Retired Michigan State Trooper Mike Stamm's contribution serves as the foreword to this volume.

Following this section, one of Hank's long-time students and close associates, Greg Phillips, with the editorial help of Jerry Proctor, has added to and updated the material Hank had completed. Greg worked with Hank for forty years studying the history and performance of edged weapons, modern, medieval and ancient, and he passes on to you many of the things Hank taught to him about knives, their history and their usage.

Interlude Contributors

- Massad Ayoob
- Richard Garrison
- Henderson Hatfield Heatherly III
- Michael D. Janich
- Nils Onsager
- John Maddox Roberts
- Whit Williams

REMEMBERING HANK REINHARDT
MASSAD AYOOB

Of all the knife-related courses I've taken over the years, none are more memorable than the one I took in Georgia many years ago with the great Hank Reinhardt.

There are historians of the edged weapons, from sword to dagger. There are master practitioners of fighting with the blade. There are experts in the craft and the metallurgy of these tools. And there are those who have actually used them to fight. To get that expertise together would normally take a large, round table of separate masters.

Or, you could just meet Hank Reinhardt.

He had devoted his life to the blade. Hank not only made his living at it, he compiled the exhaustive research that he left behind to guide the rest of us, and those who would follow later. He could design... and build... and teach... and *do*. And, perhaps more important, he could inspire.

Others could talk about *espada y daga,* but Hank could *do* it, and more importantly, he could teach it. He understood human dynamics as deeply as he did the physics of the cutting edge. Watching him demonstrate was like being in a vampire movie, where the creature of the night is in front of you, and suddenly disappears, and then reappears behind you in an instant, letting you feel that your throat is about to be opened.

He showed us what could truly be done with a blade in each hand... when to strike, and when to fall back and force the opponent to commit himself into your already-prepared defense. Hank showed us—and the world—the awesome practical value of the kukri knife, which he did so much to resurrect and popularize outside the culture that had spawned it.

Above all, he did it without ego or concern for himself. Hank taught what he did because it was important to him to continue the core value of protecting the innocent from evil.

And he lived what he taught. The day came when he flew back into Atlanta from a long knife-buying trip in Europe for Atlanta Cutlery. He didn't have his customary Star PD .45 with him under the circumstances, of course, but back then pocket knives were allowed on commercial aircraft, and he had a little folding Puma in the pocket of his jeans. Having cleaned out his refrigerator before leaving on the long trip, Hank stopped at a grocery store on his drive home from the airport.

Massad Ayoob and Hank Reinhardt.
Photo by Richard Garrison.

As he made his way back to his car with his purchases, two young punks vectored in on him in the parking lot. Hank was a slim, older guy with grey hair and eyeglasses, and apparently fit their profile of a mugging victim...a classic example of what I've come to call "sudden and acute failure of the victim selection process."

They closed into rapid contact with him and one snarled, "Give it up, old man!"

There was a soft "click" sound as the Puma's blade sprang open in Hank's right hand. His left had already grabbed the talker's belt in an iron grip, pulling him in tight to Reinhardt, who brought the razor-sharp Puma into light contact with the mugger's lower abdomen. Only then did the assailant see the confident, anticipatory grin on Hank Reinhardt's face.

The second suspect went ashen and backed away in slow motion, hands raised, an expression of confused horror on his face. The one Hank had grabbed squeaked plaintively, "No problem, old man!"

In a voice somewhere between a growl and a purr, and without losing the grin, Hank replied. "No problem at all. Ah'm gonna gut ya lak a chicken."

The would-be mugger didn't move anything but his bowels.

After a moment, Reinhardt decided it wasn't worth the paperwork, and shoved the reeking mugger away. He watched them both run...and then put his Puma back in his pocket, picked up his grocery bags, and went home.

We lost Hank Reinhardt too soon, but thankfully, much of his legacy remains. I miss him still, and I am glad that so much of what he learned, rediscovered, and created, has been preserved for us who remain, and for the generations to follow.

RICHARD GARRISON

I was still in high school when first I met Hank. It was at an early Society for Creative Anachronism event in Atlanta. I was just an observer, but nevertheless recognized Hank as someone of knowledge and I asked him about contemporary knife fighting. He asked if I had a knife and I did. I took it out, opened it and handed it over hilt first.

Hank, in a flash, reversed the knife, grabbed my shirt, pulled me in and graphically showed that I could be a dead man at that point. "The first thing," he said, "is never to give a perfectly good knife up." That was one of my first, good practical lessons that followed me through my life. Others had, undoubtedly, have learned it earlier in their life than I. But, as slow as I am, I think I am a good learner.

A few years later, I met Hank again in SF fandom. Besides science fiction, comics, the characters therein, we talked knives, swords, axes, guns... and, of course, ice tea. Like a good romance, one thing led to another and pretty soon we were shooting handguns and rifles, slashing at each other and learning about leverage and body mechanics.

My parents did a good job with me, but Hank sort of gave this Yankee a gander at some things I didn't pick up... as I wrote above, I am slow, but still a good learner.

The foremost thing I learned was the art of deception. Other attributes are good, but deception is the force multiplier to speed, leverage, timing, and strength. He understood reaction and timing like few others. He also knew how to make a person with ill-will think he had the upper-hand... until it was too late.

I also learned Hank's version of being courteous to all you meet, but have a plan to kill them.

And one of the more important lessons revolved around testosterone filled exhibitions. When you get into a friendly shooting or axe-throwing competition...and you win...shrug your shoulders like the champion you are and *don't* try to duplicate the feat, as you can only become lucky so often. Of course, a smart remark might be appropriate.

A few years later, I went from a printing and publishing background into police work. Thirty-plus years later in federal, state and local service, I still draw upon many of his strategies and tactics when I teach today. His teachings about deception were absolutely priceless when I worked undercover and later became one of the foundations for the firearms, defensive tactics, and control techniques I teach to this day.

I learned that if you were in a true-enough knife fight, you will get cut. And that pain is a series of electric nerve transmissions and you can mitigate their effects.

Hank taught me about human reaction. I learned that *action beats reaction*, but you can manipulate the outcome. He would have understood and marveled at Colonel John Boyd's OODA loop. For the uninitiated, that is an acronym for Observe-Orient-Decide-Act—an incredible, simple observation on reaction and timing. If you don't know of it, read *Certain to Win* and *Boyd: The Fighter Pilot Who Changed the Art of War.*

I learned iced tea was only proper with lime.

I learned that I was no card player, much to his disgust, as once he learned I didn't partake, a victim had been removed from the pool.

I learned that televisions can be replaced in the early dead of night and usually before Janet got home.

I learned what grief can do to a man. It can drive you to the horizon of life and, once crossed, that which you know and trust begins to be indistinct. Stray too far beyond the offing, you could lose all that it's dear to you.

Hank taught me that learning and discovery never dies.

And that this man is much bigger than his legend.

IF

If you can keep your head when all about you
Are losing theirs and blaming it on you;
If you can trust yourself when all men doubt you,
But make allowance for their doubting too:
If you can wait and not be tired by waiting,
Or, being lied about, don't deal in lies,
Or being hated don't give way to hating,
And yet don't look too good, nor talk too wise;

If you can dream—and not make dreams your master;
If you can think—and not make thoughts your aim,
If you can meet with Triumph and Disaster
And treat those two impostors just the same:.
If you can bear to hear the truth you've spoken
Twisted by knaves to make a trap for fools,
Or watch the things you gave your life to, broken,
And stoop and build 'em up with worn-out tools;

If you can make one heap of all your winnings
And risk it on one turn of pitch-and-toss,
And lose, and start again at your beginnings,
And never breathe a word about your loss:

If you can force your heart and nerve and sinew
To serve your turn long after they are gone,
And so hold on when there is nothing in you
Except the Will which says to them: "Hold on!"

If you can talk with crowds and keep your virtue,
Or walk with Kings—nor lose the common touch,
If neither foes nor loving friends can hurt you,
If all men count with you, but none too much:
If you can fill the unforgiving minute
With sixty seconds' worth of distance run,
Yours is the Earth and everything that's in it,
And—which is more—you'll be a Man, my son!

by Rudyard Kipling

HENDERSON HATFIELD HEATHERLY III

One of Hank's most attentive students bears the impressive name of Henderson Hatfield Heatherly III, a fellow of awesome height and weight who spent years as a deputy for the Jefferson County (Alabama) Sheriff's Department. "Happy," as he is known to everyone, is quick to admit: "What I learned from Hank Reinhardt saved my life on several occasions."

One such occasion came in 1981 when Happy cornered a suspect who pulled a knife and began tossing it from hand to hand as bad guys are likely to do in Hollywood films. "I had him cornered but my gun was concealed and I couldn't get to it," Happy said. "So, I did what Hank taught me: I waited until the knife was in the air, and I charged and overpowered him. Then I pulled my blackjack and wore him out."

Happy's expertise with the blackjack is exceeded only by his ability with the police baton, and that is due to hours spent with Hank fighting with sword and shield. In another incident he disarmed a knife-wielder by whacking the felon on the hand with a baton.

Hank's teachings were helpful long before Happy got into law enforcement. "In my youth a boy pulled a knife on me, but he didn't know what to do. He was holding the knife way out in front of him like thugs in the movies. So I did what Hank said and cut him on the arm," Happy concluded.

Although law officers don't customarily carry knives, they are constantly menaced by blades both sharp and dull. The problem is so common that the FBI operates a Street Survival School teaching policemen what to do when confronted by one of man's oldest weapons. Happy took the course and says he was the only member of the class who knew what to do in a certain tight situation.

"I was standing near a table when they flashed a projection of a guy coming at me with a knife," Happy said. "I ran behind the table, then drew my paint ball gun and shot him twice. Then I retreated up a stair and shot him two more times. Hank always told us to get something between us and the attacker. The rest of the class tried to shoot first and they all got cut."

MIKE JANICH

As I recall, I first learned of Hank Reinhardt through several articles that he wrote for *Blade* magazine (and its predecessor *American Blade*) back in the late 1970s. At that time, I was a teenager just getting into knives and I was impressed with Hank's writing style. It was a unique blend of well-spoken, down-to-earth eloquence, sound logic, and a wry sense of humor.

Years later, I became a both fan and frequent customer of Atlanta Cutlery and its partner business Museum Replicas. I especially enjoyed the Museum Replicas catalog since its product descriptions were much more than sales pitches; they actually provided deep historical insight into the origins, design, and function of each weapon or piece of armor. Although I was primarily interested in the Asian martial arts, through the Museum Replicas catalog I developed a much deeper understanding and appreciation for European arms and armor. Once again, the man behind that company—and the information it shared in its catalog—was Hank Reinhardt. Although I had never met the man, I realized that he had taught me quite a lot.

In 1994, I founded Paladin Press's video production department. As part of my duties as the department manager, it was my job to evaluate project proposals from potential authors and analyze market trends. For example, if there was a particular topic or book that was selling well, I would try to build on that interest by adapting it to video. Through my analysis, I realized that there was a significant interest in historical arms and armor and in the tactics of their use, but there was very little good information available on the subject in video format. From a business perspective, it seemed to be a great opportunity. From a personal perspective, I hoped it would be my chance to work with Hank Reinhardt.

I contacted Museum Replicas and asked them to have Hank give me a call. He called me the very next day and I explained my idea to him. He admitted that he was intrigued by the concept, but that he'd like to meet me and discuss it in person before he made a formal commitment. I agreed and quickly talked my boss into funding a trip to visit Hank to try to persuade him to work with Paladin.

Several weeks later, I flew to Atlanta and met Hank at his home. Walking into his living room was like entering a museum—it was filled with antique arms and armor from all over the world. Hank immediately recognized my fascination with his collection and proceeded to give me a guided tour of it in his own inimitable style. The consummate blend of museum curator and Southern gentleman, he patiently explained each piece, its origin, its combative applications, and the historical references he used to divine his information. The depth of his knowledge and the enthusiasm with which he shared it were amazing.

After several hours, Hank had worked his way through all the pieces on the main floor of his house and there was a pregnant pause in our conversation. Finally, he looked at me and asked, "Do you want to spar?" Although I wasn't sure exactly what I was getting into, I responded "Sure," and followed him down into the basement. Once again, I was amazed at what I saw. There were literally hundreds of swords, spears, axes, halberds, bows, and practically any

other traditional weapon you could think of. In the middle
of it all was a fully equipped workshop and a large open
area apparently reserved for training.

Hank knew that my background focused mostly on the
Asian martial arts and knife fighting, so he suggested that we
spar with knives. He handed me a wooden training Bowie
with a foam-padded "edge" and a fencing mask, and then
equipped himself with the same. As I donned the mask and
assumed a guard position, I wasn't quite sure what to do.
At that time, Hank was sixty-five years old and had recently
been hospitalized with pneumonia. He also suffered from
chronic respiratory problems. I certainly didn't want to insult
him by refusing his offer to spar, but at the same time, I
didn't want to do anything that would endanger his health.

Fortunately, Hank quickly "clarified" the situation. He
assumed a guard position and we touched blades as he asked
me if I was ready. I replied that I was and we both circled
slowly, sizing each other up and offering a few tentative feints.
Then, without a hint of telegraphing, he exploded forward
and hit me dead-center in the fencing mask with a snap
cut. The speed and fluidity of his movement was amazing
and it was clear that he wasn't holding back.

Since he had been kind enough to set the standard for
our match, I felt compelled to respond in kind. After circling a bit more, I feinted high to raise his guard and then
lunged forward. Stepping on his lead foot to trap it in
place, I hacked twice across his thigh and quickly backed
away. As I did, Hank stopped, looked at me for a moment,
and began to remove his mask. At first, my heart sunk as
I thought that I had offended him. But as his mask came
off, I could see that he was smiling ear to ear. He reached
out his hand to shake mine and said, "I think we're going
to get along just fine."

By the time I had finished my visit with Hank, we had

agreed to shoot a video called *The Myth of the Sword* and had laid the groundwork for a second video titled *Viking Sword*. These two videos were among my proudest accomplishments as Paladin's video producer, as they not only dispelled many of the myths that surrounded swords and their use, but they also documented at least a small portion of Hank's encyclopedic knowledge for posterity.

Working with Hank was an incredible honor and an amazing educational experience. Although his books and videos offer only a small glimpse into his broad knowledge of arms and armor, they are priceless resources for all modern students of the topic and a fitting legacy to a remarkable man.

NILS ONSAGER

Hank and I met back in the late 1980s, at the time I was jousting and a mutual friend introduced Hank as the "Sword Guy." You see, we used to fight with swords as part of our joust show and we would break them all the time. So we need a source for good swords. That was Hank.

My first visit to Hank's apartment was a little overwhelming. Literally every wall was covered with a weapon; corners were stockpiled with weapons. I was in heaven—or more accurately Valhalla. His welcoming nature and abundant knowledge were the foundation of our friendship. At the time, I had been teaching martial arts and had a second degree black belt in hapkido (a Korean form of self-defense). That first visit, we talked for about four hours, I left wiser and with a few swords.

Over the next few years, Hank and I developed a friendship. But it was more; in martial arts terms it was student and master. I had studied knife as part of my martial arts training, and Hank was naturally suspect, at the time, of the martial arts being a lot of hype. I had also spent a lot of time doing theatrical or movie sword fighting, of which Hank often said, you can't do both real and fake. He set out to prove his points and I set out to disprove them. To this day I am not sure who was right, but regardless, it shaped the nature of our relationship. There was lots of friendly banter.

Sessions with Hank were a mix of lecture, demonstration,

lab work, and sweat. After a time, I brought some of my senior students and black belts with me. Hank was a natural instructor; he taught by doing. He delighted in besting opponents half or a quarter of his age, while at the same time, teaching us. With my students, we focused primarily on the knife and we spent many an afternoon in his driveway training.

Hank's method of knife fighting was always the same but executed differently, he would win through superior aggression and speed. When I spar, I have two levels: teaching and winning. Hank only sparred with one level, winning. He always taught, but those lessons were separate from the sparring session. He believed firmly in *we act as we train*, and Hank trained to win.

This book contains many of the stories and life-lessons Hank would cite while killing you with incredible speed and jovial nature. The best lesson I learned from Hank was not one delivered in a story, but rather the way he fought. I often say, you never really know a person until you fight with them. How someone faces danger, risk, opportunity, victory, defeat, and life are all there for one to see when you fight them. I loved fighting Hank. Didn't matter if it was sword, knife, or pole axe. He was more than just a teacher to me, but rather represented the way to approach life.

In martial arts, I learned from Hank that everything sounds great, but if it doesn't work on the mat, it doesn't work. Martial arts should be a lab, not just a static set of moves. And as the world experiences changes, so must the martial arts. I applied this lesson when working on flight deck defense training after 9-11. Fighting and sparring can't be learned in books; it must be experiences, mulled around in your brain, tested, retested, and taught.

One of Hank's martial arts stories was about a karate school (I won't mention which one). They were sure they could not be touched in a knife fight and entreated Hank to spar with them so they could show him and the world. He refused for a while, mostly due to their aggrandizement. Finally, he agreed.

The fight went like this:

Their master squared off with Hank, who had a practice knife. Pennants blew in the wind. The sweat gleamed from stone features. In a flash Hank feigned an attack. The master did a perfectly timed dive roll and stood into Hank's re-positioned knife. In protest, the master exclaimed, "You can't fake an attack."

Hank taught me in the movie world to base fights on reality. I often have actors learn how to fight with a weapon before we choreograph a fight for a film. When filming a gun fight, actors must go to the range first. It makes the emotions they express so much more grounded. When I train with other stunt people, we base the fights on the real world first.

When fighting, Hank was a god. He was Mozart playing the piano. He didn't win every sparring match, but he learned and delighted in everyone that he fought with. He held honor and integrity as the virtues of being and strove to help those who were not (off the planet). When someone is gone, we idealize them, forgetting they were human, but with Hank, I remember the fights, the amazing fights.

Hank's fighting style was direct and simple. He was aggressive and adaptive. The techniques he demonstrated were obvious, after he showed them. His style of teaching became my style of teaching over the years. His style of fighting was unique. He put himself into each bout.

In life, Hank taught me to be direct and simple with a friend; be aggressive; enjoy the fight, not the victories; expect honor and value loyalty. Knife fighting should be an extension of this: Be aggressive when the fight is joined, adapt, simple is best, deception works once, and when in doubt, just smile.

The last time I fought with Hank, we were on stage at a convention. As it turns out, he was not feeling well, suffering from heart failure. But we did spar and even though it was in front of four hundred or so people, it was just the two of us alone. I luckily videotaped the entire presentation: there is no mistaking people having the time of their lives trying to kill each other.

HANK AND HIS KNIVES: A REMINISCENCE
JOHN MADDOX ROBERTS

You just couldn't separate Hank from the subject of blades. Sometimes it was swords, sometimes axes. Spears and arrows came into the conversation from time to time, since they were bladed weapons. But always it was knives. The design changed from time to time. Daggers were always there—the classic medieval fighting knife. He'd be into the seax for a while, when he was in a Viking mood. The Arab jambiyah had an inning, and he crafted a beautiful, crescent-bladed one for his own use, though he could never quite settle on a satisfactory handle for it. It was the Bowie for a short time, though Hank never developed a real affection for the classic American blade. During his last few years he was devoted to the Gurkha kukri. He went all the way to Kathmandu to get kukris and more obscure bladed items. That's dedication for you. Kathmandu, for God's sake.

I first met Hank in early spring of 1970. We'd been corresponding for about a year before that. I was in the Army and had some leave time before being sent overseas so I flew down to Birmingham to meet this guy who was into the same sort of odd stuff I was. He picked me up at the airport and we started talking as we schlepped my duffel bag out to his car. We talked on the drive into town and on the walk to his apartment and we kept on talking all that evening, grabbed a few hours sleep and resumed talking as soon as we were awake. This kept up for three or four days.

Hank's wife, Janet, later said that Hank couldn't talk for a week after I left.

Sometimes our conversation veered into exotic territory, such as the proper design for a Barsoomian longsword, since Edgar Rice Burroughs had been so sketchy with his descriptions. I'd come prepared with my drawings of my design. Needless to say, Hank had his own drawings. We discussed them vociferously. Most of these conversations took place in Hank's den or study, what would now be called his man-cave. I think Hank would have liked that term. His walls were decorated with his collection. I'd never seen so many swords outside a museum. Literally dozens. Well, maybe two dozen, anyway. This was 1970, remember.

In later years his man-cave was much bigger, constituting his whole house, actually, and he'd have to clear away that many blades just to find one book that had a reference he needed to prove some point. In these later years there arose the phenomenon of the "Hank closet." Everyone who knew him remembers the Hank closet. You opened its door at peril of your life, because out would tumble several hundred swords, bare blades and many nameless but nonetheless lethal items which you'd have to stack back inside, getting grease and rust all over your clothes in the process. He had some pretty good stuff in there, though. I still have some of that stuff.

But back to 1970. Sometimes we'd get tired of just talking so we'd go outside and across the street to a little park and there we'd fight and talk. Hank loved the sword and shield stuff, mainly because he always won. He was much taller than me, with long arms, so I never stood much of a chance. But then we'd switch to knives and I did much better, because I was in top physical condition back then, and was sneaky and treacherous. Hank was no slouch in the treachery department either, but he had the big man's arrogance while I had the smaller man's basic wisdom that you get through this life alive by waiting for the other guy to get distracted or turn his back. We'd have made a pretty good Fafhrd and Mouser team, and we talked about that, too.

I'm not sure what Hank's neighbors thought of all these doings. I guess they were used to him by that time.

We agreed that George Silver, in his *Paradoxes of Defense*, had written the best basic text on knife fighting under the heading "On ye fight wth ye single dagger" way back in the reign of Elizabeth I. The text is barely a page long and Hank had the idea of expanding it to full book length, covering all aspects of knives and knife combat, the end result of which was to be pretty much the book you are holding now. Over the years I'd visit Hank, or talk to him over the phone since we always lived so far apart, and we'd talk about his projects, which were many, and he'd usually finish with something like, "I've done another chapter on the knife book," or "The knife book is almost done, but I need to get some illustrations" or something of the sort. Now that I think of it, he may have had a presentiment that with the book his life's work would be done so he was putting it off. Sword books, in later years videos and DVDs, sure, but that knife book always remained just out of reach.

Hank never really sold me on the kukri, though he tried with the zeal of a missionary. I have the kukri he designed and gave me right here on my desk. It's a lovely weapon, but a little big to pack around. I still prefer Bowies.

Oh, and right after that visit in 1970 I was packed off to Vietnam courtesy of Uncle Sam. Hank brooded over this and was convinced that I wasn't properly armed over there. So he sent me an ax. That was the kind of guy Hank was. God, I miss him.

WHIT WILLIAMS

There are people whose abilities defy what we believe to be human. Vagueness is the fault of history and thus the feats of Milo of Croton, Egil Skallagrimsson, and the like are lost to legend. Fortunately modern history included the camera and similar technology able to prove that there are supermen and that they still walk among us. We have Bob Munden's uncanny fast draw, Howard Hill's uncanny archery, and Roger Bannister's perfect mile to name a few. I believe Hank was one of those men. He could throw an ax as accurately as most shoot a pistol. In his sixties he regularly worked out and sparred with men a third his age. But his most remarkable attribute was simply his speed.

Hank's speed had been officially tested twice in his life, once at a driving school and again by an efficiency expert. In the latter test he was found second to only Babe Ruth. In the former, his reaction time was deemed impossible. The tester actually thought his machine was broken until Hank repeated the demonstration. It had been tested in real life as well, like when he slipped under a right cross and delivered six rib breaking punches before his opponent could recover. Or another time when a pair of roughs intent on road rage pulled up loudly beside him. Hank ignored the taunts, but when he saw doors opening he knew trouble was coming. His would-be assailants never left the vehicle however. Hank exited his vehicle in a flash and slammed the door on the shin of the exiting passenger. One quick punch dispatched that one and then Hank leapt into the backseat of the convertible and dispatched the other similarly.

Speed had saved Hank's life as well. In his youth Hank hit a patch of gravel in his car once, spun out, and headed over a steep embankment. The resulting crash crushed dash to seat and surely the life out of the driver as well. Only the driver wasn't there. Somewhere in that awful descent Hank had leapt into the backseat escaping injury. Years later, while driving through Atlanta, Hank was T-boned at an intersection, the intrusion surely maiming or even killing the driver. Once again Hank wasn't there. Instead, he was sitting unscathed in the very surprised lap of his friend and passenger Sam. In a nearly identical incident, Hank's daughter was driving and was equally surprised to find herself safely in Daddy's lap having been pulled from danger by hands so fast that she didn't realize it was happening.

It is tempting to chalk these exploits up to luck and genetics, and Hank would agree that both played a role, which brings to question how any of it could be learned. Experience, however, proved to me that there was more involved.

It was five or so years into our friendship when I was driving home one night and had a disagreement as to the right of way. As I was on a motorcycle, and they in a SUV, I wisely altered course. Unfortunately my new direction was toward a guard rail and beyond that a precipice not unlike the one Hank had faced. I tried to steer out of it but my tires hit the curb at an angle, dumping bike and rider hard to the pavement—only the rider wasn't there. Instead I was standing safely by looking down at the damage. You see I had jumped off the bike. This wasn't a planned action, in my wildest dreams this solution to a crash had not occurred to me. Nor was it lucky panic. I saw what was happening, consciously let go of the handlebars, placed both hands on the gas tank, did a big push up off the bike and hit the ground running. I couldn't help but see the comparison with Hank's experience.

There were other signs as well. I am famously clumsy and am known for dropping fragile things and knocking over beer bottles with gestures of my right hand. I am also known for catching them before they hit floor or bar. The thing about this is that I am not particularly fast. In fact I am probably the slow man on the fight team. Some of my other opponents beg to differ, but the camera doesn't lie, and I demonstrate no remarkable velocity in movement. No, it isn't the speed of my movement; it's the learned lack of wasted effort.

Hank was an avid reader and possessed a collection of all things martial that rivaled any common library or bookstore. Despite that there was only one book that Hank credited with directly affecting his fighting style. Not the well worn copy of *The Book of Five Rings*, nor the well loved sagas of Iceland, it was the novel *Cheaper by the Dozen*. Now, if you've read this good work you should realize that it was not the Gilbreth's fertility that was of interest, but their professions. They were pioneer efficiency experts and liked to measure tasks in therbligs. A therblig is a single motion and the fewer therbligs used the more efficiently the task was performed. Well, sparring Hank was a study in minimalism and efficiency. When you cut at Hank he did not dodge, he did not parry, he simply wasn't where you thought he was. And on the opposite end there was no wind up, no tell of motion; hell, there was rarely any motion perceived, just the sting of a rubber knife on your hand or the sound of it bouncing off your fencing mask.

Not long under this tutelage I became aware of how slow the rest of the world seemed to move. Like one of the many times a patient came up off of the stretcher swinging. This particular patient was in good shape for having been on the losing end of a knife fight. He was fortunate to have only minor wounds but was covered in blood and high on adrenaline. My fellow EMT was the real speed demon that day, having uttered the offense that aroused our offender and then promptly exited the ambulance faster than I had ever seen him move. In the meantime that bloody fist seemed to take forever in its course, and when it finally got there I wasn't. I let it pass me by and then grabbed the offending shoulder and continued its owner's motion around and out the side door. My philosophy here was that he would either realize he needed my help or bleed out enough to become manageable, either way I could wait him out. As it turned out Atlanta's finest had just arrived and I had thrown him into the arms of a large officer who promptly threw him back at me. A couple of rounds of ping pong later and the patient became manageable. I looked out to see what had become of my partner and spotted him across the street far enough away to be calling for the back-up that had already arrived.

Stories about the mean streets of Atlanta were something Hank and I shared, he having lived in them, me working them. But there were far more insidious things in them to worry about than fists. I was placing EKG leads on a patient sitting on his front porch when someone down the street decided they had a score to settle with him or his friends, or possibly just had a pathological dislike for medics. In any case when the shooting started I am proud to say I was the first behind cover. But it didn't seem that way at the time. I remember looking up at the noise and distinctly noticing that there were at least two guns involved, one with the high pitch of a small caliber rifle and the other the low thump of a large caliber pistol. Then I noticed pieces flying off the porch around me and a peculiar sensation of hot tingling on my face which I can only describe as the sensation of awareness of vulnerability. It then occurred to me that perhaps I should get behind something and I stepped into the open door of the house. Meanwhile my partner hit the ground hard enough to injure himself and the patient experienced a remarkable recovery and fled the scene. Two things I learned that day was that Churchill was right and that time really does slow down. Only it wasn't the way I had read about it. There was no tunnel vision, there was no panicky motion, I had all the time in the world and used it wisely.

About a year later, and half a world away in Baghdad, a rocket came screaming past my clinic one day (rockets, by the way, are loud and terrifying in a way you just have to experience to understand, but it's mortars that keep you up at night for the opposite reason in that they don't have that polite warning of direction) and in one smooth motion I was under my desk, pistol and vest in hand.

Just south of this in a slightly friendlier neighborhood I had been attacked by a group of disgruntled locals. I had a lucrative position at the time and feared deportation so I refrained from delivering an immediate pummeling and went on the defensive. Easily avoiding both fist and foot and whipping agal (the fan belt that accessorizes Arab headgear), I kept my eyes on hands and waist looking for the danger: the dreaded jambiya and the Middle Eastern tactic Hank had taught me to watch for. This was a grab of the shoulder, a knee to the groin and finally a knife to the throat. Neither materialized and I quickly realized I had little to fear from this assault. They apparently got that point as well and gave up, freely going on their way through a country that rarely prosecutes offenses to foreigners.

Hank was glad to have me back Stateside but I was sad to see that in his seventies youth and skill might finally catch old age and treachery. We last sparred about a month before he went into the hospital. We paired off with rubber knives in his basement and in one explosive move I reached out and cut his right hand. But before I could congratulate myself I received a cut across my throat from right to left. Right to left! Yes, I had cut his knife hand—but the knife was no longer there. Hank had treacherously swapped it to his left hand and I never saw it coming.

PART II

Greg Phillips

FOREWORD

I have been interested in edged weapons, and edged weapons combat, for as long as I can remember. Fortunately for me as a young boy, Hank Reinhardt moved into the apartment next to mine. Hank liked to tell the tale of how he first met me—that I was squatting in the brush next to a fire with one unknown piece of meat on a spit, flaking a stone point.

And in Hank's book of short stories that he and Jerry Page put together, *Heroic Fantasy,* he wrote, "And I gave him the gift of steel." Actually this is a great exaggeration but still not far from the truth. This was back in the day when if you wanted a shirt of mail you damn well had to make it yourself. This project and others put me on a long and interesting path learning the history of how weapons were made and used.

This book is a history of knife combat. As in all such histories, there are some graphic details in this book. This is a book about how it was. Not a how-to book. Neither

Hank nor I are suggesting that you cut your hair into a duck tail, put on too-tight blue jeans, buy a vintage Springer switchblade, and start searching your local alleys and bars looking for a rumble. But there are lessons to be learned here. What Hank taught me was, "The best fight you will ever have is the one you never get into."

In all histories of warfare there are many distasteful scenes and descriptions. If this book were about the atom bomb and the horror of its use at Hiroshima, I wouldn't suggest that you build a bomb and blow up a major city to see how it works. Nor are we suggesting here that you use the information in this book to engage in grisly knife combat. I hope you enjoy this work of history as much as I have enjoyed being able to put it all together.

—Greg Phillips,
Birmingham, Alabama, 2011

7

CHOOSING A KNIFE

Knife design has advanced considerably since Hank Reinhardt practiced it in the 1950s to 1970s. I first became aware of this as a teenager, when I saw Hank flip open a knife one-handed, a stunning feat in those days.

Is this a switchblade, I asked him? He introduced me to the lock-blade knife and showed how the trick was done. Nowadays this is no big deal, with companies manufacturing knives with blade assists like buttons and loops. With almost no practice you can equal the speed I achieved as a teenager—and with no cut thumbs either.

Mercator, one-handed operation thumb groove.
7¾ inches overall length. From the collection of Greg Phillips.

Al-Mar folder, 7 inches overall length.
Photo by Oleg Volk. HRC648

When I was a kid, one of the ways to modify a pocket knife to speed one-hand opening, was to stick a bolster—a matchstick, or two toothpicks—in the handle of the knife to partially raise the blade and make opening easier.

The knife would be bolster-down in your pocket, and in theory you would grab that knife and the point would snag on your blue jeans as you drew it, and you would impress all with this lightning-fast one-handed opening. The first time I ever saw this done, I really didn't think it was that good a trick, and years later I can tell you the major disadvantage of opening this way.

I was sitting on a loading dock with a number of my coworkers, and I had to cut the plastic band off a box. I pulled out my knife and opened it one-handed, which was kind of a surprise to some of the guys. At the time, this was not the kind of thing that a clean-cut boy was supposed to be able to do. Immediately one of my coworkers said he was a lot faster using his method of opening as opposed to mine. He had a yellow handled Case pocket knife and had bumped the blade up with two matchsticks. I returned my knife to my pocket and told him to "beat this." Now we had a crowd, and with a crowd comes some pressure. With a

Circular mechanical assist, 7½ inches overall length. HRC629

certain element you just "ain't no man unless you can get your knife out."

We had a foreman say "go!" He went for his knife and I went for mine. I hate to admit, but he did time me dead even. I looked over at his face and I saw a look of surprise. I then realized that it was not the surprise of tying me on a knife-drawing contest, but the fact that on the draw he had managed to cut a two-inch-deep, four-inch-wide gash across his ass.

ASSISTED OPENING TECHNIQUES

These days, there are basically four ways to open a knife one-handed. We have the Spyderco thumbhole system; the thumb stud and levers at the top of the blade; assisted opening; and switchblades or automatics. Let's get the switchblade subject out of the way. There are several current manufacturers of switchblades. Some are quite good, but the one thing they all have in common is that they are mechanical. The most important thing about a weapon is reliability. Anything that uses a spring to make it open, whether it be a flat spring, or a coil, or a cold spring, can break, or get clogged with pocket junk. This means it won't open when you need it the most.

On top of that, the only switchblades I've seen with any speed are those with coil springs. The rest are slow and

Spyderco, 8½ inches overall length. HRC250

Precursor to assisted opening knife with button lock,
circa 1980, 7 inches overall length.
From the collection of Patrick Gibbs.

noisy. As Hank pointed out earlier, sometimes it is best to open your pocket knife quietly. It's best for your opponent not to see or hear it. This isn't possible with a switchblade. They are either opening loudly with a great deal of speed, or not at all.

The best thing to do is to keep it simple. There are just better choices for a pocket knife than automatics.

Now let's talk about assisted opens. You might call this a geriatric switchblade. It opens quickly but you have to help it. This is the worst of both worlds. The only advantage I can see here is one of legality. It isn't an illegal switchblade, but then in its action it almost is—but on the other hand it might keep you out of the slammer.

Next, we have thumb studs: this is probably your second best way of one-handed opening, but it still lags far behind the Spyderco hole. There seems to be a new gadget coming out every day for opening a pocket knife one-handed. By the time this book is printed, who knows what new inventions we will see. But keep these things in mind—the

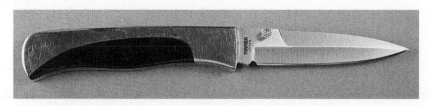

Knife with thumb stud, 9¼ inches overall length. HRC621

most important advantage of any knife, or for that matter any weapon, is that it must be simple and reliable. This is especially true when someone is under stress. So ask yourself: how well will any new design perform if your hands are cold, wet or injured? How quickly and well can you get this knife into operation?

At this time, I think the best thing out there is a Spyderco with the wave feature. As you draw the knife from your pocket, this small hook grabs the cloth of your pocket and snaps the knife open. You can do this with cold hands, wet hands, and arthritic hands. At this point I think this is the best and fastest pocket knife on the market.

Who would have ever thought that the hole in the top of a blade, a simple yet ingenious design, would change the knife world as we know it? This was the first attempt to design a knife that would open one-handed that everybody could use. Once this trend started it launched a tidal wave of gadgets for opening blades one-handed, some good and some not so good.

Spyderco Wave, 7 inches overall length.
From the collection of Greg Phillips. Photo by Oleg Volk.

CLIPS

While we are on the subject of fast operation, let's talk about pocket clips. The big advantage of clips is that you always know where your knife is in your pocket. This helps make for a fast and smooth draw. Also, with your pocket clip, you

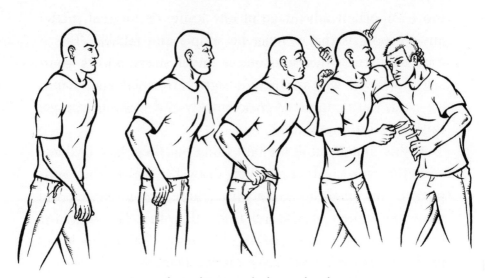

A pocket clip can help make for a
fast and smooth draw from your pocket.

need to be able to move the clip from one side of the knife
to the other. For all you left-handed guys, when you look
at your knife, make sure that you can move the clip to left
or right side, and from top to bottom. This is a tremendous
advantage if you carry a gun on your right side, you can
still have your knife available for a left-handed draw.

Now for the disadvantages: All you have to do is look
at somebody's pocket and you can see a knife clip there.
There are many times when you don't want anyone to know
you have the knife on you. That's why you need to have
a pocket clip which is removable. With a removable clip,
you can have a deep concealment draw of your knife. You
don't want anything to snag the blade in your pocket. For
the deep draw you need to take the clip off.

Spyderco was the company that introduced the pocket clip.
This small little strip of steel now means that your pocket
knife is always in the same position and you don't have to
either dig through the change and other pocket detritus to
find your knife or sew your pockets, as Hank suggested.

The only disadvantage is that there are times you do not want anyone to see you have a pocket knife. The answer is simple: remove the pocket clip (easily done with a small screwdriver) or you can simply leave the pocket clip on but let the knife rest in your pocket. Try both methods and see what works best for you.

I know I am sounding like a salesman for Saul Glasner, but with a combination of the pocket clip and the wave feature, you can even draw your knife from a seated position. Once again, ladies and gents, this does take practice. But to date this is the fastest gadget I've seen to get a knife out of your pocket lickety-split.

The whole point of a knife is its edge (no pun intended), of which there are basically only two types: serrated and smooth. There are a lot of advantages to a serrated blade. It rips through a lot of material even wet stuff, wet rope, or seat belts—this is where serrations really shine. The biggest disadvantage is limited life expectancy; they can only be sharpened a few times, then they lose their effectiveness. I cannot tell you how many knives I have ground the serrations off of, and put a straight edge on, to extend the life of the knife. When you pay over forty dollars for a knife, you want to get as much use out of it as you can.

The other disadvantages of serrations include that they are hard to sharpen and that the cut of a serrated knife is not as smooth as those of a straight edge, especially if the serrations are dull.

Then we have the worst of both worlds, the half-serrated and half-straight, the knife which cannot make up its mind. This is how you can take a perfectly good design and get a knife that won't do well at any task. In addition, it is a hair-pulling operation to sharpen. So either get your knife serrated or with a straight edge. Don't buy one in a state of confusion.

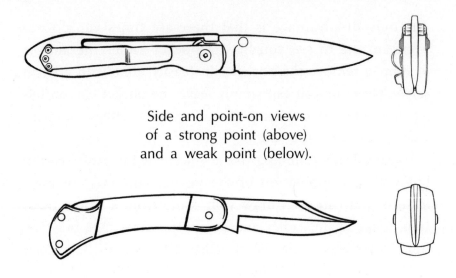

Side and point-on views
of a strong point (above)
and a weak point (below).

BLADE GEOMETRY

Now for blade geometry. Basically a knife is a wedge. If it's too thin, it will wedge in the material. If it's too thick, it won't penetrate the material. You might have an extremely sharp edge with a hollow ground profile. The disadvantage here is the more you sharpen it, the less hollow ground it becomes. We know pocket knives are thin, but you would be surprised how much better they cut with the right geometry.

Plus, a hollow grind on a knife results in a not very strong shape. It chips easily and can develop cracks which will create breaks. I once saw a high quality hollow ground pocket knife that had about two inches of the blade gone. Somebody had cut an individual in a denim jacket. He hit a button on the jacket and lost two inches of blade on a pocket knife which was not very large to begin with. The remaining blade didn't give him much to work with. Instead of a hollow grind, we need a shallow "V" shaped blade with not a whole lot of really sharp point. But the point needs to be as strong as the edge: remember, your opponent may have change in his pocket or ball point pens, or a coat with heavy buttons or zippers. The point needs to be strong enough to hit these items and still skate off to puncture him. Trouble is, it's difficult to find a pocket knife with a strong point. They are naturally thin by nature. Pick designs with the strongest points.

TESTING THE CUTTING EDGE

Nowadays, almost any brand of pocket knife you buy is shaving sharp right out of the box. Of course, as with all weapons, you still need to check the edge to make sure it is that sharp. This needs to be done carefully, and I must emphasize, *really,* carefully.

Take the knife, put it on your arm, raise it to a 45-degree angle with blade just touching the skin, then carefully push the knife towards your hand in a shaving motion. This takes practice.

If the knife is truly sharp, the hair should literally jump off your arm. As a self-defense pocket knife, your weapon should be this sharp at all times. The first time I ever saw a shaving-sharp pocket knife, Hank was cutting off a shoe-lace that had gotten frayed. He literally touched it and cut through it. This is one of those you-had-to-be-there things. I told Hank I had never seen anything cut that quickly. At this point Hank said, "Let me show you something." We went to the bathroom and Hank lathered up just below one of his uneven sideburns. Then he proceeded to shave his face to even up that sideburn. That knife was as sharp as my grandfather's straight razor.

I asked Hank if he could show me how to make my knife that sharp. He said he would show me, but that if I cut myself I shouldn't "come crying to him." That same day I brought over my prized possession, a small four-inch bladed

Case sheath knife. After much trial and error, I was able to get that knife so that it would shave hair off my arm.

I used to think this was as sharp as you could get a knife. That was until Jimmy Fikes, a nationally known bladesmith, returned to the Birmingham area, and showed me a whole new level of sharpness. I can now take a paperback book and cut the ends off that book by simply pressing down with hand pressure.

The knife world is really in love with the new, different, and exotic. As with serrations, the tanto point has become all the rage. This is rather amazing and got me considering that the Japanese knife we know as "tanto" does not have this point style. If you look at the rounded point of most pocket knives, you will see they have basically the same cutting effect as the tanto point. There are those who say that it will penetrate better than other point styles, better than a round style knife. You can easily discover the truth by doing the old stab-the-phonebook test. You'll find that the tanto point penetrates no deeper than the round point style. If you want a sexy and svelte pocket knife, by all means get a tanto point but don't expect it to perform any better than Grandad's point style.

In the twenty-first century, most new knives will be shaving-sharp when you get them. If a blade is this sharp and will cut easily through a small paperback book, no

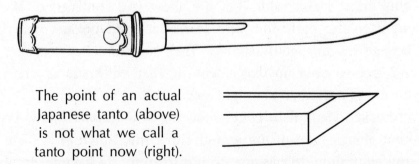

The point of an actual Japanese tanto (above) is not what we call a tanto point now (right).

more sharpening is necessary. However, part of this job is mental. You must think of your pocket knife as a weapon, not a tool. You can cut a little string here, cut a cardboard box there, maybe open up a package, and your edge is no longer shaving sharp. I suggest you don't use your knife as a tool. That way your edge is always ready to defend your honor.

STEEL

Current steels are an important subject. Just a few years ago most stainless steel pocket knives had some of the poorest edge-holding qualities this side of a junk yard.

I had a name brand pocket knife given me by a friend. After sharpening a pencil, it would go from hair-flying sharp to so dull that you could apply pressure on the edge with your thumb and it would not even bite the skin. Now, there are several specialty melts of stainless steel that now hold an excellent edge. I recently tested a Cold Steel pocket knife that cut a hundred pieces of half-inch sisal rope, then carved one paperback book into small pieces, and afterwards was still sharp enough to shave hair on my arm. Hopefully one day we will see a production knife that will cut two hundred pieces of one-inch Manila rope, slice a paperback book and then be able to cut the tips off standing hair on my arm. The more the public learns about knife sharpness, the better the quality of knives we will see.

More recently Spyderco and some other manufacturers have been using a stainless steel called VG-10. The edge-holding ability of this stainless has been excellent. I have been able to cut a hundred pieces of half-inch sisal rope and the knife still has a good working edge. I have recently been testing a knife from Diamond Blade. They use a process called friction forging. I was extremely skeptical of this new tempering process, but like the bank robber said to Dirty Harry, "I just gots to know." This knife was book-cutting sharp right out of the box. The first cut on the rope was so easy I thought I had bought rotten rope. I made three hundred cuts on the half-inch sisal and I was still able to cut the end off a paperback book just using light pressure on the spine of the blade.

I have not used any production knife which will equal this performance. I'm looking forward to seeing larger knives from this company. It just goes to show that the possibility of almost legendary performance can be had from a production knife.

I've also tested a laminated blade from Cold Steel in their Natchez Bowie style. This uses a combination of two stainless steels forged together in a sandwich. The edge-holding ability was excellent right out of the box. With a helper feeding me rope, I cut a hundred pieces of manila rope at a speed so fast it was a miracle I did not start a fire in my backyard.

Ladies and gents, if we continue with these new tempering techniques and laminated steels, we may very easily see a knife offered from a factory that will cut a thousand pieces of one-inch manila rope, and when placed in a vise will take a 90-degree bend and return to true.

So keep in mind, when we talk about blade steels—don't be hung up on what type of steel is used in the knife. Just stick with the performance.

8

ACQUIRING BASIC SKILLS

You've chosen a pocket knife. You know the edge is sharp. Now we need to warm up. Take your knife in your master hand (right or left) and begin to slowly open the knife. The reason I say "slowly" is because even with our newer designs, trying to master this skill too quickly will earn you cut fingers and wounded pride. So take your knife and slowly open it. Then put the knife in your left hand and begin to open it with your left hand and pass it back to your right. Take your time. If you continue to practice this routine soon you can open your knife as fast with either hand. It is very important to be able to use both hands, so if your master hand is injured you will not be put out of action.

So, step one, open the knife right-handed, pass it over to your left and open it left-handed. Pass it back to your right hand and continue this swapping until you are proficient with both hands.

PRACTICING THE CUT

Now it's time to practice some cutting. A good practice target is a cardboard tube that comes with paper towel rolls. Stand the tube on a flat surface and practice cutting it in two with one fast slice. You must be cautious here. Make sure all your body parts—feet, hands, and knees—are out of the way. Cut at a 45-degree angle, which will pin the roll for a second and will allow you to cut the tube in half. It is possible to be fast enough to cut the tube in half and still leave the bottom part standing. This is tricky. I have been able to do this about once in thirty tries. But the more you practice the easier it gets.

After you can sever the tube with your right hand, it is time to start practicing with your left. Keep working your lesser hand until it is as proficient as the master hand, then it's time to start practicing drawing the knife from your pocket. Once again, start out slowly. Don't try for speed at first. Make sure your draw is fumble free. Once you master the smooth draw and smooth opening, it's time to start practicing drawing the knife from your pocket and cutting the cardboard tube in one motion. Keep in mind that yanking the knife out too fast, and then having it go sailing through the air, creates a loss of much face. So keep it slow and keep it simple until you've mastered the technique.

Cutting a tube; before and after. Photo by Casey Ferguson.

The next cut you practice will insure blade alignment and speed. Get a large package of notebook paper. Take one sheet of the paper and fold it over to make a pyramid. Stand the pyramid on a table or counter about waist high and practice cutting it in half. Not only is this difficult to do, but it is very difficult to get the paper to stand on its own. If there is an air conditioner or heater going, or someone moving in the room, the paper is easily blown over. This trick requires an extremely sharp

Cutting a rope; before & after. Photo by Casey Ferguson.

knife and a lot of speed. The angle of the knife must be just right. It is possible to cut the two pieces of paper in half and not have the bottom portion fall over. I've only been able to do this about twice in a thousand tries.

Now it's time to test both strength and speed. Find some half-inch manila or sisal rope. Hang it off a limb or swing set in your yard and practice making three very fast cuts. First slash at the right hand side of the rope. Then, cutting from left to right, make three more very fast cuts as well. Practice this until you get even, fast cuts on the rope. But don't forget safety. Remember you are swinging viciously with a very sharp instrument. Keep your hands, knees, and legs well out of the way.

PRACTICING WITH THE POINT

Now that you've mastered speed cutting with the edge, it is time to consider that the pocket knife has a point as well as an edge. Take a plastic soft drink bottle and fill it with water. Place it at about chest level and try to make three quick thrusts before it falls over. Don't just try to stab wildly at the bottle. Put a mark or a one-inch-square piece of tape on it and aim for that spot. Practice drawing the knife out of your pocket and stabbing at the spot. Continue to practice until you hit the spot. Once you can hit it (or close to it), try to increase your speed. Keep the same tempo as you did with the manila rope. This is also true when we cut the rope. Plastic bottles are easy to find, cardboard tubes come with paper towel rolls, and manila rope can be bought at hardware stores. They are good, cheap practice materials that can die many times for your improvement.

Now that we have gotten to the point that you can draw your knife and smoothly stab an object, let's talk a little bit about footwork. Alleys are full of junk. They are dark, bumpy, and slippery. Your own backyard is also. You can't count on your knife fight occurring in a perfectly maintained gymnasium. So be aware of your surroundings. The best way to avoid tripping over junk in the road is to retreat by taking a step back, then pulling your other foot back to you. It is also the best way to travel, when moving either left or right, to keep from getting tangled in your own feet.

Practice these moves: step backwards until you run into a wall, then step forward and left. Step backwards until you run into the wall again, then step forward and to your right. This is awkward at first, but once you get the feel of your own feet it becomes second nature. But I emphasize again doing it slowly until second nature kicks in.

Next, go outside and practice your newly acquired footwork. Take along some bottles, paper, and a bag of garbage. That way you will get the feel of junk on the ground. It is very important you learn how to remain standing in difficult terrain. A smart opponent will try to maneuver you into cracks on the ground or into garbage. I suggest you do this to them before they do it to you. If you can maneuver yourself until your opponent falls, it is much to your advantage.

I once saw Hank do this very thing in a practice fight where the area featured some bushes and a creek behind his opponent. He maneuvered the individual to the edge of the bushes where he made a fast hard lunge, at which point the opponent stepped back out of the way. We heard a large scream and the opponent ended up waist-deep in water and covered in mud. When we went down to the creek to help him up, he looked up at Hank and said, "If I didn't know better I'd think you did that on purpose."

Hank looked up at me sternly and said, "Greg, what do you think about that?"

I looked back at Hank and said, "One of the first things you ever told me is that there are no rules in a fight."

These are wise words to remember. When knives come out, play time is over. Keep this in mind: you do whatever you have to do to win.

SPARRING

There are several companies that make suitable knives for sparring. You can pick one of these or you can make your own. One of the simplest and cheapest simulated knives is a rolled-up newspaper. Remember this has to duplicate the length of your pocket knife. So measure your knife and make sure your newspaper is no longer. Just roll the paper

A rubber Fairbairn-Sykes.

Sparring knife Hank weighted with tape and lead weight to give it the heft of a real knife. Photo by Casey Ferguson. HRC630

tight, but not too tight, with just a little bend to it. Make it roughly about an inch-and-a-half in diameter, and bind it with three strips of tape. Duct tape or masking tape work well.

Now that you have your sparring knives, mark a line on the bottom sides to position the edges, so when you cut you won't be cutting with the "flat" of the newspaper.

You will need some kind of eye protection. There are several commercial brands of sports glasses that can work with this. Also, a full-coverage helmet is not a bad idea. It is difficult to practice using a weapon without picking up some kind of injury. You can reduce the amount of suffering involved if both you and your partner spar carefully and obey whatever rules you pass to govern this activity. I used these paper knives for years with Hank and was never injured. This was not just luck. It had a lot to do with two people who sparred frequently and who knew each other's moves. You can establish the rule of no-facial-cuts with your opponent, and if you work well with each other you won't have to worry about black eyes and missing teeth at the end of your session. (Note that Hank did not like to do this because it leads to a lack of head defense.)

When beginning the sparring, keep in mind that pocket knives are short, so you will be working very close to your opponent. This creates several disadvantages. It means your

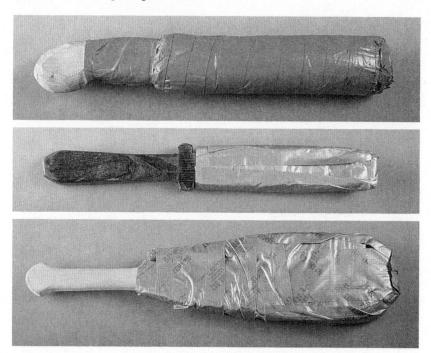

Top to bottom: a sparring Bowie,
a sparring knife with wooden handle for dagger,
and a sparring kukri.

arm can be locked into position, your opponent can close with you and take you to the ground; you can be kicked, punched, and even bitten. This is where consistent and rapid motion comes to your rescue. You must be in motion most of the time, preventing your opponent from coming any closer and drawing a bead on some part of your anatomy.

Start with your paper knife in your back pocket. Let your opponent have his knife in his hand. On the "go" signal, your opponent should be about two yards away when he attacks. This will teach you footwork in getting out of the way, plus improving reaction time in drawing your knife from your back pocket. Now swap and let your opponent assume your role as you attack.

When you attack, deliver a snapping type of a cut that is very fast, but is done with minimal power which is ideal

The Reinhardt
Snap starts
as a punch.

for pocket knife use. This is not unlike a jab in boxing. We call it the "Reinhardt Snap."

This is an excellent cut to maim your opponents' hands, forearms, neck, and face. If your opponent's hand sticks out far enough from his body, then make this fast, snapping cut at his hand. If the throat is exposed, make the same cut to the throat on either the left or the right side. This is a very quick snapping cut in and out. If you can get enough small cuts on hands, forearms, throat, or legs—with minimal danger to yourself—you will come out a winner at the end.

Then practice the sweep. That's using your non-knife hand and forearm to push your opponent's knife out of the way. This is very tricky stuff but if well-timed can be a real winner. Quickly step in and use your non-knife-holding hand to drive your opponent's knife hand away from you. Quickly close with your opponent and cut him across the carotid artery in his neck, then step back out of the way equally fast. This move also can be done by sweeping your opponent's knife hand to one side and striking the inside of his arm. Then as you close, stab your opponent quickly in the groin. Once again you must be in and out quickly.

There is a great deal of danger to both these moves, but with practice they are hard to beat.

If your opponent closes with you, you are not easily able to make a cut. This is where sawing on your opponent comes in handy. The best places to use your knife in this situation are the tendons behind his leg, on his ankle, and under his armpits. This is also an excellent method if somebody grabs you and takes you to the ground, where you have no room to stab or try another type of cut. The method is simple: put your knife on a joint of his body and with all the pressure you can muster, saw back and forth. Hopefully, you will get an artery or a tendon which immobilizes him. If nothing else, he will want to turn loose of you and that is what you want him to do. This is why we need to have continuous motion. Try not to let your opponent close with you—keep moving to the left and right, backward and forward.

The slashing cut has great merit. The areas we want to attack are the top of the forearm, on the upper inside of the biceps, the stomach, and inside the thigh. This is a little slower than the Reinhardt Snap but covers a great deal of damage area. A slash on the collarbone all the way across the body to a man's bellybutton, about an inch-and-a-half deep, will just about let you go home smiling. Once again: in and out quickly. This can be left to right, or right to left, across either side of the neck. You can close in, make this long slash, and pull out. But there's a lot of exposure to you on a cut like this. It's much better to break your opponent down with the Reinhardt Snap than to risk a long slash across your opponent's body.

While we are on this subject, let's get rid of this crap about "just taking the cut." If your opponent has a sharp knife,

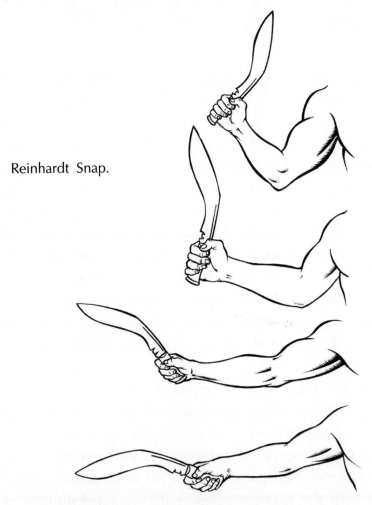

Reinhardt Snap.

A snap cut to the neck.

the first cut you receive probably will be your last. There are times that maneuvers like a sweep or an arm lock may expose you to a cut, but to intentionally throw your arm up to block a cut, and to take that cut across your forearm, is a quick trip the loser's corner. It's all about speed and maneuverability, not letting your opponent chop you up.

THRUSTING

The thrust is a very effective but dangerous move with small knives. You must get perilously close to your subject to make it work, and much of your body will be exposed during the maneuver. Recall that with pocket knives there isn't much blade to work with. You also have to worry about what you might hit when you suddenly strike out at an opponent. The rib cage and sternum present a lot of resistance. As discussed above, other objects like zippers, big iron buttons, and the clutter people carry in their top pockets can deflect or even break the point of your knife. Your target area is limited, so thrust below the sternum, moving in and out extremely fast.

Your throat, forearm, and stomach are all immediately exposed during a straight line thrust. But at the same time your opponent presents you with some choice targets: the front of his throat, the inside of his arms, the inside of his thighs, and his groin. The ability to hit these small areas will depend in large part on the amount of practice you expend and the speed and consistency you develop during these practice sessions.

Most importantly, you must not telegraph the fact you are about to thrust or the direction that thrust will take. Practice in front of a mirror might reveal damaging clues, or "tells," which could enable your foe to dice you up before your thrust can get underway. A thrust is not unlike the Reinhardt Snap. One needs to explode into a rigid stab, then pop back out of the way. Once again this is easy to practice. Set a water filled plastic container at about chest height and mark a target on it with a one inch square piece of duct tape. When you are poised and ready to make strike, have your sparring partner say "go!" then thrust and try to hit the small piece of tape. Once again start slowly, and with practice build up speed. The most important thing is to be able to hit the tape consistently. Once you have acquired accuracy, then work on speed.

So, you have worked at it and have both speed and accuracy down pat? Now take the knife and conceal it in your pocket. Then practice drawing your knife and thrusting at the piece of tape. Once again start slowly and cautiously.

Make sure all of your body parts are safely out of the way—hands, arms, legs, etc. Make sure your footwork is correct. You need a strong, wide foot stance, so that you are in no danger of slipping or sliding. This practice also helps you measure distance correctly, so you will know how close you need to be to an opponent before thrusting.

9

FIGHTING WITH THE BIG KNIVES

Hank picked three big knives to represent this whole category: the Bowie knife, the kukri, and the dagger. He felt that this trio of cutting weapons generally covered the whole field.

KUKRI

First we have the kukri. The first time I saw this type of weapon, it was a picture, not the actual knife. I was sitting

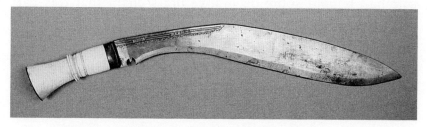

Nepalese kukri, 18.5 inches overall length. HRC42

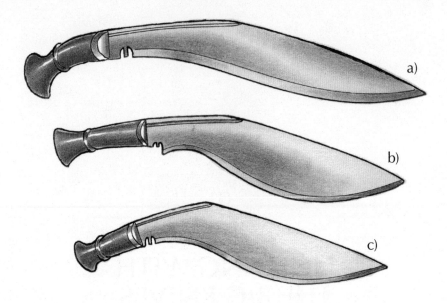

The three basic forms of the kukri:
    a) the Sirupate kukri favored by the Limbu tribe,
    b) the Bhujpore style favored by the Rais,
    c) the standard kukri favored by the other tribes.

Illustration by Peter Fuller.

in Hank's den looking through *Stone's Glossary* of weapons. I noticed this large knife with an unusual shape. I asked Hank if he had ever had a kukri, since I didn't see one in his collection. He told me the last kukri he had, he had bought overseas, and that it had terrific cutting power. He laughed and said he found out how well it cut because his wife had bought some decorative brass chain that was part of a curtain set. The chain was too long, and he did not have a hacksaw to cut it off. So he took it outside and laid it on a two-by-four board and cut the chain in half with the kukri. He was really surprised at how easy the chain was parted. Out of curiosity he did it again on the leftover end piece. It cut the second time as easily as it did the first.

After our discussion about the kukri, Hank told me he

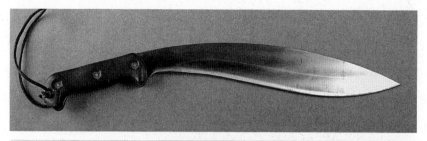

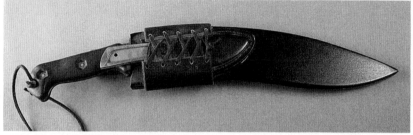

Reinhardt combat kukri, in and out of its sheath.
17½ inches overall length. HRC649

would like to get another for his collection. Little did we know at this time, but the kukri would put him back in touch with Bill Adams, and the two of them would conspire to create Museum Replicas Ltd.

For ages the kukri has been both tool and weapon to the Gurkha natives of little Nepal in the Himalaya Mountains between India and China. Many Gurkhas have fought for the British Army since the nineteenth century and covered themselves with distinction for their fidelity and deadly skill with the kukri.

In World War II the Gurkhas slashed a bloody trail through the German Army in Italy's Arno Valley. In one encounter, while cleaning Germans out of farm houses, Officer Jemanadar Bakhandho Rai killed six Germans and Jemadar Harkajit Limbu accounted for another five, all with kukris. Two German tanks which were advancing were leaped upon by the Gurkhas and their crews sliced to pieces.

So don't let anyone convince you the kukri is not a

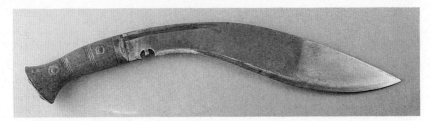

M43 World War II Kukri, 17 inches overall lenth.
From the collection of Greg Phillips.

legitimate weapon of modern war. As a weapon the kukri has much to offer us. It provides length, speed, and power.

Kukris come in a bewildering array of shapes. Basically we will separate the types by saying there are vintage kukris and modern kukris. Atlanta Cutlery still offers a military issue kukri. On this you pay your money and you take your chances; it is a work in progress. If you are handy with hand tools, with a little elbow grease and a little grinding, you could produce a pretty good weapon.

There are a lot of vintage kukris floating around, some from World War II, and some a little older. There are also some current manufacturers who make an excellent product. One example is Cold Steel. They manufacture an excellent standard Limbu-style kukri, similar to a Bhujpore shape.

In the days of the single-shot rifles, kukris were very large, many of them exceeding fourteen inches in length. As repeating firearms came into vogue, kukris shrank, to

Current issue kukri with wooden handle, 15 inches overall length. From the collection of Greg Phillips.

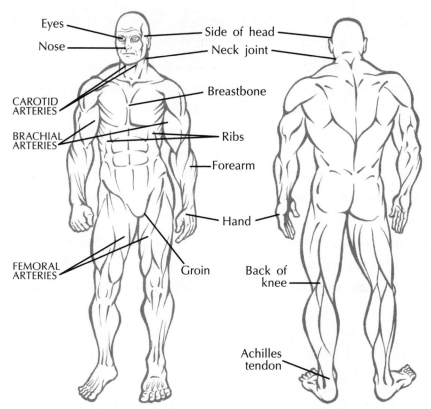

Best kukri target areas on the human body.

an average of twelve to thirteen inches. At these lengths a tremendous amount of cutting power is still available. Suddenly our target areas begin to change. It is possible now to chop into the upper part of an opponent's forearm and not just cut through to the bone, as we did with a pocket knife, but to shear all the way through the arm.

Never doubt that the kukri is a modern weapon. Recently a band of about forty robbers traveling on a passenger train in West Bengal, India, started stealing jewelry, cell phones, and cash. A Nepalese soldier had about all of this he was going to put up with, especially when a group of robbers began to molest a young girl sitting next to him. He began attacking them with his kukri, and he killed three and injured

eight others. Even in the modern world, a highly motivated
mind and a sharp knife can still prevail.

You are not just cutting fingers now with the Reinhardt
Snap, but you're cutting fingers off. Your target now expands
past the soft portions of the throat and includes the side
of the head all the way down to the point where the neck
joins the shoulder. We can now slice through the clavicle
and into the body. The back of the knee is just an annoy-
ance with a pocket knife, but with the kukri you can now
put an opponent on the ground with one cut.

All the moves we talked about with the pocket knife are
considerably more deadly once we go up in size. There are
those who say the kukri is no good in a thrust, but with

Thrusting with the kukri.

the proper hand hold on the grip, we can now drive straight forward with a hard thrust and shear through the breast bone or ribs. It is definitely not the best design for a thrust, but it can work.

Now let's talk about our training procedures: Again fill a large plastic soda bottle full of water, and practice until you can cut the top off just below the cap. Do this with a kukri and the Reinhardt Snap. Practice this until you can cut the top off without knocking

Whit Williams cutting a water bottle. Photo by Kevin Gravitt.

the bottle over. Then we will try to cut slightly below that area, and cut through without knocking the bottle over. Cut at an angle. This holds the bottle to the surface and keeps it from falling over. This is also true when one tries to cut an opponent. It is a lot easier to cut "with the grain" and not against it.

Now that you have worked on speed, it's time to work on power. Take a one-inch piece of manila rope and hang it vertically. Practice until you can cut this piece. Practice safety at all times. Always wear eye protection and make sure no body part is out in front of your cut. Keep legs and hands out of the way. Remember, this is fighting, not ballet. Style note: no matter how much you scream it will not help you cut through this rope. It also will be a waste of time to have a "war face." No matter how much you holler and frown, this piece of rope is still going to be tough to cut.

Once you have achieved one cut, try to make two fast ones on the same piece of rope. Once you have cut two pieces fast, it's time to go on. Take two pieces of one-inch manila rope and tape them together at one-foot intervals.

Tape them tightly. Now your target area will be the piece of tape holding the rope together. Cut through either the piece of tape or slightly above it. This is good practice for speed, accuracy, and power.

FIGHTING SITUATIONS

These practice techniques assume you will be standing up and able to maneuver. In this case, you face your adversary, flick out with the Reinhardt Snap and cut your opponent across his hand or forearm. This should cause your opponent to lose control of his knife hand, enabling you to step back in and chop him across the carotid arteries on either side of his neck. This move must be done quickly, in and out with great speed, and never forgetting proper footwork.

You face your adversary, he thrusts at you. Using your superior footwork, you step back out of the way. As your opponent is fully extended in his thrust, you cut him across the brachial artery. (That's the big artery on the inside of the arm, running from armpit to hand.)

Once again this must be timed perfectly. You need to watch the shoulder and arm of your opponent to make sure he is fully committed to a long thrust. If your opponent tries to cut you across the forearm or hand, step back out of range, and when he is fully extended, slash him across the forearm, then quickly skid up into the throat, severing his carotid arteries.

If your opponent tries to cut you across the carotid artery, bend down and get beneath the cut. Once again this needs to be practiced in sparring. As your opponent's knife goes over your head, chop upward in a hard slashing cut, into the groin or the femoral artery, then immediately glide back out of the way using smooth and even footwork. This is

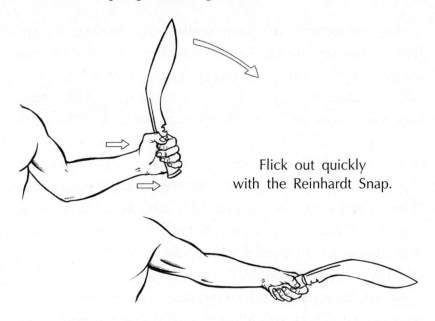

Flick out quickly
with the Reinhardt Snap.

extremely dangerous because you expose a lot of your body, but if properly practiced and executed it is hard to beat. The femoral artery lies just under the skin at the groin and is easy to sever. Also, a cut in the testicles causes painful discomfort. Most anybody chopped there will be ready to clock out and go home.

Keep in mind this works better if your adversary is the same height as you or taller. There's too much danger if he is shorter than you, because you are exposed much longer to your opponent's cuts. Quickly size up your opponent. If you are taller and have longer reach use these to your advantage. It's not a good idea to close with a shorter man. But if you are shorter than your opponents, try to close the gap quickly and get inside his guard.

But say you face an opponent who has a hammer, piece of pipe or any similar striking instrument. As he raises the instrument above his head, flick the kukri out and cut him across the carotids. This move must be perfectly timed, and that takes practice. As the very instant he has his weapon over his head is when you must strike.

Now for some seated fighting situations. Say you are sitting in your automobile. An individual tries to force his way inside. There's no room to swing or chop with a kukri in a car. Now take the edge of your kukri in a quick movement, and draw it back and forth across your assailant's forearm in a sawing motion. This should make him yearn to turn loose of you or your steering wheel immediately. If he doesn't, then give a short quick jab to his face with the point. Your aiming point is his nose or eyes. This should get the response you want. Then immediately drive off. Remember, your foe may have a friend nearby who could try to force his way into the passenger side.

As you have gathered by now, inside an automobile is a poor place to chop with a kukri. That's where you need the knife's inwardly curved edge to saw, and its point to stab. This is true, too, outside the car when an opponent closes with you and perhaps grabs your clothing. Use that inward curve to saw him across the neck, the inside of his thigh, behind his knee, and across the Achilles tendon of his ankle.

These are your basic moves for fighting with the kukri. You and your sparring partner should practice them until both are perfect in both maneuver and timing. Later you can add variations as you practice, in case your opponent comes up with surprise threats we have not mentioned. Remember fighting skills are like a pyramid. What I have given you here is just the base of the structure. The point of the pyramid is up to you and the only way you will get there is to practice these moves to improve speed and timing.

BOWIE KNIFE

The first time I ever saw a large Bowie knife, I was whittling an extremely hard piece of hickory into a spear. I had fire-hardened the point and was laboriously scraping it when Hank walked up and asked what I was doing. He looked at the point and said, "Let me see that." And he started shaving it with his pocket knife. He looked up and said, "The hell with this. It's taken the edge off my knife." He disappeared into the house and returned with his Randall Smithsonian Bowie. In about ten seconds he managed to chop a very serviceable point on that hickory, which saved me a lot of work.

I had seen Bowie knives before in the windows of pawn shops, and of course who could forget the movie *Iron Mistress*? This was the very first time I had seen anything actually cut up with one. This knife is truly America's gladius.

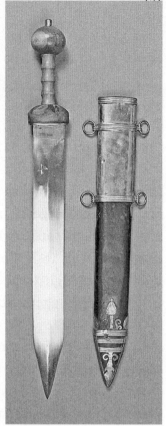

Reproduction gladius, 28 inches overall length. HRC218

For this book, we'll define a Bowie as a knife four inches or longer with a clip point and a sharpened top edge. The ability of this weapon as a tool of carnage is legendary. So much so, that it is still outlawed in many Southern states.

Legend has it that the first Bowie knife was crafted about 1827, by an Arkansas blacksmith/knifesmith named

Blade by Jim Fikes, 14 inches overall length. HRC647

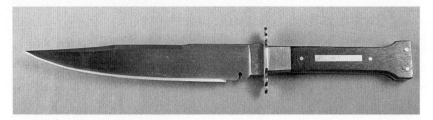

Modern reproduction Bowie, 14 inches overall length. HRC129

James Black, according to the specifications of Alamo hero
James Bowie. Legend insists that a Bowie knife had to be
sharp enough for shaving, and heavy enough to use as a
hatchet. It had to be long enough to be swung as a sword,
and wide enough to paddle a canoe. This description might
be slightly exaggerated, but there is no doubt the Bowie
was a large knife with a blade sometimes fourteen to eigh-
teen inches long. It was soon the object of tall tales and
legends from Virginia to Texas.

As with the kukri, as repeating weapons proliferated, the
knife became a secondary weapon and got smaller in size.

The most highly publicized story of its use occurred at
the first session of the Arkansas General Assembly in 1837.
A bill offering bounties for wolf hides sparked an argument between Rep. Major J. J. Anthony and House Speaker

A historical Bowie; the blade alone is 14½ inches long.
From *The Antique Bowie Knife Book,* Charles Schreiner III collection

John Wilson. After several insults were tossed at each other, Wilson descended from the Speaker's platform. And when they reached the bottom step each man drew his Bowie knife.

Perhaps in hopes of averting a fight, someone shoved a chair between them. But Anthony and Wilson each grabbed a part of the chair in his left hand and began slashing with his right. Anthony cut downward at Wilson's left wrist and almost severed it from its arm. He then threw his knife at Wilson, but it failed to strike on its point and fell to the floor. Wilson then thrust his knife to the hilt into his foe, and Anthony collapsed and died a few minutes later.

Wilson was arrested, expelled from the House of Representatives, but later was acquitted in trial on the grounds of "excusable homicide." It was bloody episodes like this that energized Southern legislatures to outlaw the Bowie knife.

There are also several states where a great many knives are illegal due to blade length and design. Before you carry any knife on your person it is up to you to contact your state attorney general's office and determine the exact wording of the law. Don't follow the advice of some potential jailhouse lawyer, or the opinion of a friend who says, "They told me it was okay." Don't even pattern your knife-carrying habits upon what you read in the newspaper, or watch on television. Do your research and find out the facts.

Now, here are some choices for a current Bowie knife. One that Hank and I both had fondly desired is Randall's No. 1. This is an excellent choice; probably the best is the

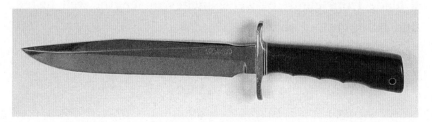

Randall No. 1, 12½ inches overall length. HRC601

seven- or eight-inch blade. This knife is fast with good point speed and, although hollow ground, it has a good deal of edge toughness. It can be bought in several different handle styles from stag to Micarta. In addition, an excellent, high quality sheath comes with the purchase.

Another fine example is Cold Steel's Laredo Bowie. On the ones I've tested so far, the factory edge has been book-cutting sharp. It is a well designed knife with good handle qualities and a very strong flat grind. If you are fairly tall, six feet or above, it's very easy to carry a Bowie knife in the twelve-inch length. But if you're shorter, one of seven or eight inches is the better choice.

The custom world is full of Bowie knives. You can afford to be choosy. The next time you talk to a custom knife maker, you need to sound him out on these subjects: Will your knife be tested before he delivers it? The test should include flexing the blade and watching it return to true. Edge-holding ability should be tested as well. Your custom blade should cut a hundred pieces of one-inch manila rope without going dull. You should be able to drive your knife into a hardwood board without bending the point. You should be able to cut through a two-by-four plank at least three times, and the handle should be tightly mounted afterwards.

If your custom bladesmith's knife won't pass these tests, then it's better to find someone else's work that will. If you must tote a Bowie, then stick one in your sheath with a blade from eight to twelve inches in length, well tested, and book-cutting sharp.

FIGHTING WITH THE BOWIE

When it comes to fighting with your Bowie, you are well armed. Like the kukri in the previous chapter, you have tremendous cutting power at your command. If your knife is well designed it should have terrific point speed. You can achieve deep penetration, wider wound tracks, and the ability to move in and out very quickly.

As you face your adversary, you can beat him to the cut by using the Reinhardt Snap, slicing him across his fingers, the inside of his forearms, or the top and outside of his wrist. Also, a lightning quick thrust to the opponent's hand is now possible. Driving the point two inches into his wrist or hand is a good start. Equally neat is a quick thrust to the inside of his thigh, using the sharpened back edge of the Bowie and using the arterial illustration for your key targets. A lighting quick straight line thrust to the front of your opponent's throat, or a quick snap cut across the carotid arteries of the neck—these are some of the moves that make the Bowie a superior fighting tool.

If you miss a cut, you can easily snap back underneath to cut your opponent's forearms or inside his thigh, by using the Bowie's back edge.

Some suicidally inclined antagonists have committed the folly of trying to snatch a Bowie away from a foe by grabbing that long blade. This is a losing game if the

Human arterial system.

back edge is properly sharpened. If someone grabs the top of your knife, give it a quick twist to the left, then yank it backwards, breaking his grip and cutting his palm.

Now that you are aware that your Bowie can cut in both directions, practice this in your sparring. But don't neglect additional practice with inanimate objects. In the previous chapter we used the kukri to slice water-filled jugs. Practice this with your Bowie as well. Get out your length of free-hanging manila rope, and blaze away with the Reinhardt Snap, whacking off pieces of rope until the act comes easily. Now stack two water-filled soda cans and practice cutting

Snap back underneath to cut the thigh.

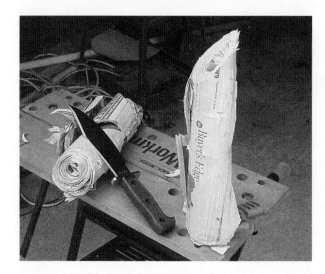

Practice with your Bowie until the art of cutting comes easily. Photo by Whit Williams.

the top one in half without turning the bottom one over. You can also roll up newspapers.

Remember, the only way to learn how to cut is to cut. You need to constantly practice to keep your strength and speed up.

And while you are keeping yourself in shape, don't forget the health of your knife. Test your Bowie knife constantly by cutting free hanging rope. Keep both the point and the edge sharp, And if you buy a custom blade make sure the bladesmith has cut through at least one two-by-four, and has flexed the blade at least 24 degrees out of line and seen it return to true.

THE DAGGER

Now, for man's oldest self-defense knife: the dagger. I don't think there is any shape that has been praised or cursed as much. Critics of this shape will tell you it's not very strong, that it has very little cutting power. But you need to look at the dagger not as a tool but purely as a weapon. The point isn't very strong if you try to lever up rocks, or dig up roots

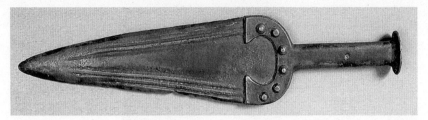

Reproduction bronze dagger, 11 inches overall length. HRC175

with it. But if used for its intended purpose, the dagger is one of the most versatile fighting designs.

It can be forged very light and thin, which makes it a joy to carry. It has the ability to cut in either direction. It's very difficult to snatch a well-shaped dagger from somebody's hand; a pyramid shape is hard to hold onto.

EVOLUTION OF THE DAGGER

One of man's oldest fighting knife shapes is a piercing weapon. It doesn't matter whether it was made of wood, stone, or metal. Its advantages are many. In the early era of armor, a dagger-shape point would push through links of mail, and in a later period easily through the visor of a knightly helmet.

The dagger shape is primarily an awl-style with two parallel edges and it makes for a wonderful fighting blade. The ability to cut in many different directions expands your attack and defense in different ways. So, not only can it be used as a

Reproduction medieval baselard, 14¾ inches overall length.
From the collection of Jerry Proctor.

penetrating weapon, but properly designed and sharpened it makes an excellent tool as well.

Many early daggers were of bronze. Although bronze is an excellent material, it still has many flaws. Its inability to withstand shock is one of them. Even with this drawback, it is more than strong enough for excellent penetration. As we progress to the era of iron and steel, the ability to cut with a dagger shape becomes a reality. A very common medieval shape, the baselard, is an example of strength in both its ability to cut and penetrate. This blade was so popular that it was celebrated in poems, as you can see from the example below. (Okay, not *great* poetry.)

> Lesteneth, lordyngs, I zou beseke,
> Ther is non man worst (worth) a leke,
> Be he sturdy, be he meke,
>   But he bere a baselard.
>
> Myn baselard hazt a schede of red,
> And a clene loket of led,
> Me thinketh I may bere up my hed,
>   For I bere myn baselard.
>
> My baselard hazt a trencher kene,
> Fayr as rasour scharp a schene (bright),
> Euere me thinketh I may be kene,
>   For I bere a baselard.

(FROM THE ERA OF HENRY VIII. SLONE MSS)

Swords often influence knife shapes. As the rapier became a fighting sword of the late medieval period, the dagger developed into a companion fighting blade in its purest form. With the elaborate hand protection to help facilitate parries,

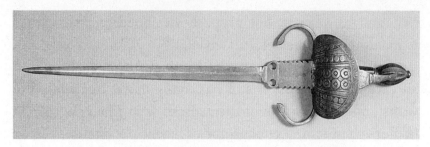

Reproduction main gauche, approximately
24–25 inches overall length. "Main gauche"
means "left hand" in French. HRC121

you see development of the elongated guards enhancing the ability to protect the left hand.

The dagger as a fighting knife has never slowed in its development. An excellent modern example is Randall's Model No. 2. At the beginning of World War II, knifemaker Bo Randall received a sample of the Fairbairn-Sykes fighting dagger. As legend has it, Bo threw the knife into a hard local palm tree, and about half an inch of the point snapped off. Bo felt he could do better.

Also it's quite possible that there was a great deal of input on this project from Colonel Rex Applegate. The truth of the combined effort of these individuals is somewhat lost in the mists of time. Randall's final product was an extremely strong, well-designed dagger shape which developed a cultlike following. From the lowest-paid GI to the highest ranks of the U.S. military, it is still celebrated today as an excellent example of a dagger.

All fighting knives have advantages and disadvantages. Let your surroundings be your guide. As there is a vast difference between a Ferrari and a tractor, fighting knife shapes vary similarly according to their use. For example, if you are heading into a jungle environment, a kukri is an excellent choice, but not a dagger. Try to pair your weapon with the terrain.

During World War I, a dagger-shaped knife, roughly about

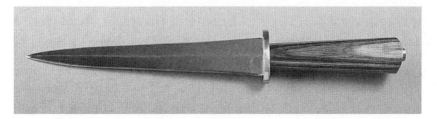

Randall No. 2 kit blade, hilted by Hank Reinhardt,
12¾ inches overall length. HRC603

five to six inches in length, had been issued to German troops. Later on this same shape with a metal clip-on sheath had been reissued in the Second World War. This was a handy way of concealing your dagger under your clothes or in a boot top.

There are several reproductions of this same dagger still available. It is as good a choice today as it was in 1918. Boker Knives produces this item now. I have stabbed this reproduction into an oak chair top with no bending of the point. Neither the handle scales nor the guard loosened. Right out of the box its blade cut a hundred pieces of half-inch sisal rope without going dull.

I don't think there is any dagger style more cursed or blessed than the Fairbairn-Sykes Fighting Knife. This double-edged dagger was made famous during World War II through its issue to British Commandos and the nascent SAS. It is still available from many sources today. And used for its intended purpose, as a weapon not a tool, it is a pretty good fighting instrument. I recall back in the day Hank used to talk about

A reproduction Fairbairn-Sykes with a metal grip,
11½ inches overall length. HRC612

going to a surplus store in Atlanta in the 1950s and seeing a barrel full of Fairbairns, different models in various kinds of sheaths, for twenty-five cents each. Boy, have things changed. Now these same knives are selling for $950 to $1,000. Needless to say, this puts them in the high end collection category and out of the cheap carrying category.

You can still get a good Fairbairn reproduction, and they vary greatly in quality. I've seen some from Sheffield Cutlery and Flatware of England that were so hard that one could break the point off by merely flexing it. I've seen others so soft that they would easily bend by applying a light pressure to the point. Once again, the only way to determine the quality of your knife is to test it.

TESTING THE DAGGER

Put on your safety glasses. Place a paperback book on a table, and put the point of the knife at a 45-degree angle to the book and press down to flex it. Your knife should bend and return to true. Then flip the knife over and repeat the process on the other side. If the knife hasn't taken a permanent bend, take two paperback books, one on top of the other, and stab into both books, point downward. Here is where you could put that icepick grip to good use. You should have a great deal of penetration. Both the guard and the handle should be intact and not loose.

Once you have tested your dagger, make sure the edges are sharp on both sides. It's impossible to test a dagger for book-cutting sharpness because of the double edge. However, you can check the edges by seeing if they are shaving sharp. If they are, you are raring to go.

Down through the ages the dagger has been a real whiz-bang in combat and assassinations. Those who consider this knife style as romantic and impractical should consider this story told me by a naval aviator in World War II. His plane was shot down during a sea battle and he quickly found himself floating in a sea full of desperate Japanese soldiers, victims of a nearby troopship sinking. Our hero had on the only life vest available in that part of the Pacific Ocean, and immediately large numbers of Japanese paddled in to take it away from him.

Our aviator stood them off with a .45 automatic until he ran out of ammunition, then he yanked out his dagger boot knife and began stabbing in all directions. He managed this startling stabbing feat because his dagger was secured to his arm by a lanyard. Without it the Japanese could easily have taken the knife away. He continued stabbing and pushing bodies away until he was rescued by a passing destroyer.

If there are any doubters left as to the dagger's usefulness, consider this story told me by a German soldier, survivor of the frigid Russian front in World War II. As a member of the SS, he had spent a great deal of time on the Eastern Front, where his type was cordially hated by all Russians. My friend and his companion, both tired and cold, were dragging a load of supplies on a sled. They apparently were spending more time looking forward than looking around, because suddenly he was staring down the barrel of a PPsh submachine gun, with two Russian soldiers gazing back at him.

A prisoner on the Eastern Front—not a nice situation under the best of circumstances. My friend cursed himself for his stupidity in not keeping track of his surroundings. Life immediately got much worse than it had before. The Russians piled their own supplies on the sled and made the Germans drag the double load.

The other German soldier had been sick for several days and began coughing and falling down in the snow. The first time he fell, the Russians beat and kicked him to get him back up. He arose and pulled the sled a good distance, then he fell again. This time one of the Russians shot him through the head.

Now my friend knew his goose was really cooked. He struggled to pull the heavy sled, and along the way he began to hatch a scheme. He was wearing three pair of pants, and in the first layer stuck in a pocket was his boot knife. He knew if he fell in the snow the Russians would begin to beat him, at which point he could reach in his pants, pull out his dagger and stab at least one Russian, leaving the odds even. This was a dangerous proposition: they might beat him until he was unable to run, or they might just shoot him. But at this point he would rather be shot than spend the rest of the war in a Russian prisoner of war camp.

He noticed a small stand of trees about a hundred and fifty yards away and this made up his mind. The snow was much harder in that area, making for better footing. So he deliberately slipped and fell down.

When a Russian swinging a Mosin-Nagant rifle came over to beat him, he exploded out of the snow and stabbed the Russian twice in the groin. Then he ran like hell to the shelter of the trees. The other Russian began chasing him and did not stop to take aim—my friend hurled insults over his shoulder to keep the Russian from stopping. He reached the shelter of the trees and the Russian didn't follow. That thoughtful fellow returned to the sled and mercifully shot his stabbed companion in the head.

There are some important points to be made here: being able to have a concealed dagger can save your life. And being able to thrust into the right target area, very quickly, is the only way to carry it out. He who hesitates is dead meat.

DAGGER TECHNIQUES

Let's talk about some fighting techniques that are easy with a dagger. This blade shape doesn't have much cutting power, but it is very quick. It is capable of a fast thrust to your opponent's forearm or hand. And it cuts in both directions, so a missed cut can be redirected as a reverse slash.

The dagger adapts easily to tricky counter maneuvers. For one: as your opponents slices at you, bend over at the waist

Because a dagger can cut in both directions,
a missed cut can be redirected as a reverse slash.

and let his blade go over the top. At the same instant stab upward into his groin or the inside of his thighs, hitting the testicles or the arteries on either side. This is an especially easy move if your opponent is taller. But timing is crucial and it takes a great deal of practice. I would suggest that when you practice your sparring partner wear an athletic cup. It is wise to save all our injuries for the real knife fight.

Another cut is a direct line thrust to the side of the head, right below the earlobe. You need to close with your opponent, make a sweep across his forearm, then make a direct

When you practice, your sparring partner
should wear an athletic cup.

line thrust, and step back out. This move presents a lot of exposure to you, but properly executed it gets the job done.

One big advantage of the dagger is that hand cuts can be delivered in almost any direction. If your blade is under your opponent's hand, all you have to do is cut upwards. If you are above your opponent's hand, a cut in almost any direction will make contact.

A dagger is one of the most difficult weapons to snatch

When properly executed,
a direct line thrust to the side of the head,
right below the earlobe, is effective.

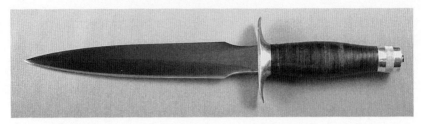

Randall No. 2, 12¾ inches overall length. HRC618

from an opponent's hand. With edges top and bottom it is almost impossible to grab the blade without being severely cut. Always be sure you blade is extremely sharp, and that the profile of your blade extremely thin. Your need a very sharp point, but not a thin one. It's easy to see how this can be accomplished by looking at a Randall No. 2. It has enough weight to have cutting power but it is still light enough to make a fast, snapping cut, with a point that is strong yet sharp.

In choosing a dagger shape, make sure that your choice fits this profile, you'll have a dagger that can both cut and thrust. Extremely thin needle type points are not necessary on a modern fighting dagger. We are not worrying about piercing a mail shirt, or a doublet full of whalebone.

With a strong point design and a lot of distal taper, the ideal design can be moved with amazing speed. Quick straight-line thrusts even to the sternum have a good chance of penetration into the thoracic cavity and beyond. Also, snapping cuts like the Reinhardt Snap are easy with this design. Daggers may be out of style with some current notions of knife fighting, but you can have one of the best weapons ever designed in your hands.

10

YOU, THE KNIFEFIGHTER

MINDSET

Of all the weapons you may carry, the most powerful and versatile is your brain. And of all the attitudes one may carry, alertness is often most useful. Be alert to your surroundings at all times. You are especially vulnerable going in or out of your home or going to and from your vehicle. No one can be hot and ready to go twenty-four hours a day, seven days a week. But in times of heightened danger you need to kick it up a notch. Little things count—like when entering a building, locating the exits and observing the walls which might cover your rear should you suddenly face an encounter.

This is something difficult to teach, but if you have the habit of constant awareness you are less likely to be surprised and panicked by a sudden attack. Keep your hand unobtrusively on the knife in your pocket when going to and from your vehicle, or your house. Of course, alertness isn't all of it by a long shot. To survive an encounter, you must develop a certain mindset which is even harder to teach—the will to survive and the determination to overcome. Hank discussed the warrior's mindset in his book on swords.

But to summarize it here: Begin this process by paying attention to your looks. If a person looks like a victim, walks and talks like a victim, and carries a victim's mindset, the kindest way to describe this person is what we lovingly call the "whining weenie." He is usually the priority target of every mugger and thug in the neighborhood.

A friend of mine had a coworker who fitted this character perfectly. He was scared to death of his own shadow, and he asked my friend for ideas to protect himself. My friend suggested he buy a gun and learn to shoot it. His response was one of horror: "Oh, my God they're expensive and make a lot of noise when you pull the trigger. The mugger will just take it away from you."

My friend suggested he get some pepper spray instead. His response was equally stricken: "What if it doesn't work and they beat me up?"

My friend then suggested he buy a knife and learn how to use it. His response: "My God, what if they take it away from me and stab me with it?" I think you are beginning to get my point. No amount of training or equipment will help this guy. He had short-circuited his strongest weapon, his brain. General George S. Patton, Jr. said it differently: "Do not take counsel of your fears." If this is your attitude about defending yourself and your family, I guess you are just going to end up being a victim.

If a confident appearance and awareness of your surroundings still aren't enough for you to avoid combat, there are other attitudes to cultivate. First, it is important to stay one step ahead of your opponent, no matter how deadly the encounter. Second, fix in your head the idea that you are going to win no matter what occurs.

Now that we have discussed your mental attitude, keep in mind one of the best ways to avoid trouble is to treat everybody just the way you would want to be treated. This is not a book about manners. But being a gentleman at all times will keep you out of a lot of trouble.

PHYSICAL TRAINING

Almost as important as the knife-fighter's mindset is his physical training. If you are faster, stronger, and more durable than your opponent it is a definite plus. Sitting on a couch reading this book, while avoiding any physical exercise, can quickly put you on the casualty list. It is not necessary to buy a total gym and try to become the new Mr. America. One of the cheapest and simplest methods is to buy a set of five-pound hand weights. Begin by doing twenty-five curls with both arms. Then raise the weights to chest level, and do twenty-five jabs with the right hand and twenty-five jabs with the left. Take a five-minute break. Then and do fifty jabs with the left, fifty jabs with the right, followed by fifty curls with both hands.

After a ten-second break, do a hundred curls and a hundred jabs with both hands. Rest for another ten seconds, then repeat the process. Keep this up for thirty minutes. Do this every day. You will soon find your speed on the jab has improved greatly, and your arm strength has improved too. This simple exercise can be done almost anywhere, for only the cost of two inexpensive hand weights.

Now for a quick review: Choose your knife carefully. Beware of gimmicks. Practice your cutting on cardboard, free-hanging half-inch manila rope, and water-filled soda bottles. Practice the draw from your pocket until it is smooth and fast. Mesh your draw and cutting with proper footwork. Get on your weight routine and stick to it. Find a good group of sparring partners and practice often. And remember, have a winner's mindset.

SHARPENING YOUR BLADE

In several of the chapters we have talked about the sharpness of your knife. In our first chapter we referred to shaving-sharp edges. This is self explanatory. You take the edge of the knife and put it on your arm at a 45-degree angle and push forward. The knife should shave hair from your arm. You need to be very careful when you do this. Go slow!

We have often referred to "book-cutting" sharpness of a knife. Just take a paperback book, lay it on a flat surface, and with your hand along the spine of the knife, you push down, rocking the edge left to right. If your blade is really sharp it should cut through the book with no trouble at all. Be careful. You can really cut the hell out of yourself.

We also talked about cutting free-hanging rope and water-filled soda cans or bottles. You should cut through the rope at a 45-degree angle and the bottles as well. Once again be very careful. To really cut well you need to practice often and keep all body parts well out of the way

If your knife is dull and won't cut books or shave, you'll need to sharpen it. Remember that sharpening is just the removal of metal. It doesn't matter how you do it as long as you get results. One of the easiest ways to do this is to take a diamond hone or hard Arkansas stone and follow the bevel of your knife up and down. Once you run the stone down one side of the bevel, on the opposite side you will in time feel a "feather" or "burr." Then repeat the process on the other side of the knife, and you'll feel the same thing there. Now buff this feather off by stropping the blade back and forth on a buffing block. This block can easily be made by gluing a strip of leather to a block of wood. About five inches of a two-by-four works just fine.

What does this feather or burr look like? Often it is big enough to be seen by the naked eye. As you buff the blade on the block, look at the edge under magnification and you will see a little silver hair along the edge line. Once this hair is buffed off, you need to continue to buff until the edge is book-cutting sharp. This takes a great deal of practice, but once mastered it can be done with a diamond hone and the belt right off your pants,

This method requires no tools at all, no belt sanders, no buffing wheels. Occasionally buffing the edge of you knife between cuttings is the easiest way I know to keep your knife in top condition. Make a buffing block and remember to keep your edge sharp. All it requires is practice, lots of it. Don't get frustrated. Like Mama's cornbread, just keep doing it until you get it right.

THE TRUE SECRETS OF KNIFE FIGHTING

Hank Reinhardt was a true student of edged weapon combat, so much so that he traveled around the world seeking knowledge in this field. One of his trips took him to the roof of the world, tiny Nepal in the Himalaya Mountains, home of the Gurkhas and the kukri. On his return I asked him what he had discovered.

He told me he had traveled the dusty mountain roads to a small Nepalese village. One of the inhabitants there was a highly decorated Nepalese soldier who has used the kukri to good effect on many occasions in many battles. Hank met this pleasant gentleman on a cold, wind-swept pass and asked him if he would mind discussing his battle exploits.

The Hillman smiled and said he would be glad to recall the years he fought for the English king. Hank asked him, "How best do you use the kukri in combat?" The Nepalese answered back in a thick accent:

"It is best to use the edge of the kukri, because that is the part that cuts, sir."

Hank nodded his head in agreement. "Now that we've established that you use the edge of the knife to cut with," Hank asked, "how best do you use the edge of your kukri?" The Gurkha smiled and replied:

"You hit them with the edge very hard."

Hank inquired further, "If you hit them with the edge and it does not work, what do you do then?" The small Hillman looked at Hank as though he had lost his mind and answered:

"You hit them again—harder."

Hank then wanted to know if there were any other useful moves with the kukri in combat. The Nepalese replied with a grin:

"If you hit them with the edge and hit them hard, then that is all that is necessary."

After Hank told me this on the telephone there was a brief moment of silence between both of us, and then I said to Hank, "Let me get this straight: I need to use the edge of my knife, because that is the sharp part. If that doesn't work, then I hit them again—is that right?"

"Well, tiger, I guess that's the way it goes," Hank replied.

At this point we both broke out laughing. You see, there are no real secrets to fighting with knives. There are only good sharp edges, well-honed points, lots of practice with

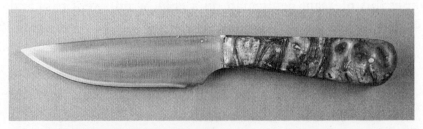

Knife by Jlm Fikes, 10 inches overall length. HRC602

good sparring partners, and using your mind to beat your opponent. But then again, that's the way we always knew it was. And you don't have to go to the roof of the world to find it out.

ABOUT HANK REINHARDT

Hank Reinhardt was a widely known authority on medieval arms and armor. He wrote numerous articles on swords and knives for the magazines, and his book on the use of the sword was published posthumously in 2009 titled *The Book of Swords* (Baen Books). He produced two videos with Paladin Press on the sword, and appeared in *Reclaiming the Blade* and other documentaries and TV shows about swords. In his last years of life, he was a columnist for *Blade* magazine on swords in the movies.

A sword and knife buff from early teen age, Reinhardt received an education in both during Army service in Europe in the 1950s, visiting famous museums. Upon returning to the United States, he worked at various jobs before meeting Bill Adams, founder and president of Atlanta Cutlery. With Bill, Hank was a cofounder of the mail-order business Museum Replicas, Ltd., and later a consultant to many sword makers.

He has received numerous awards for activities in science fiction and for his work with bladed weapons, including the Industry Achievement Award given at the 2006 *Blade* Show in Atlanta.

Unlike many experts, Reinhardt insisted on actually making and testing the weapons he wrote about, and through his various activities he has been instrumental in increasing the popularity of arms and armor in mainstream America.

ABOUT GREG PHILLIPS

I met Hank Reinhardt when I was a ten-year-old kid, and he introduced me to the world of weapons and armor. He taught me the mysteries of swords and knives and how to use them—always cautioning me in the iron restraint one must always maintain when using such dangerous objects.

Hank bestowed an encyclopedia of knowledge on me— knives and how to sharpen and use them; the secrets of swordplay and unarmed combat; the history of weapons and armor.

Later on I met Jim Fikes and he taught me how make these weapons. Fikes is the undisputed maestro of the bladesmith's forge and from Jimmy I got one of the finest educations in the secrets of Damascus steel and how it is produced, plus the knowledge of knife edges that are beyond sharp.

Many of the lessons I learned from Hank have helped me survive more than thirty years in private security. This book is about those lessons. I hope you enjoy reading about them as much as I did learning them in my youth.

PHOTO CREDITS

Knife class, by Richard Garrison.

Hank and his knives, by Richard Garrison.

Hank at Dragoncon, by Nils Onsager.

Flint knife, by Charlotte Proctor.

Nepalese kukri, HRC 45, by Suzanne Hughes.

Arab jambiya, HRC 516, by Suzanne Hughes.

Fighting knife, HRC 43, by Suzanne Hughes.

Standard folder, HRC 617, by Suzanne Hughes.

Historic Bowie, from *The Antique Bowie Knife Book*, reproduced by permission of Bill Adams.

Reproduction Fairbairn-Sykes, HRC 612, by Suzanne Hughes.

Typical pocket folder, HRC 616, by Suzanne Hughes.

Concealable boot knife, HRC 32, by Suzanne Hughes.

Hank's Queen, HRC 650, by Suzanne Hughes.

Grab the wrist, grab the back of the guard, photos by Elizabeth Arthur.

Hank Reinhardt, by Greg Phillips.

Massad Ayoob & Hank Reinhardt, by Richard Garrison.

Mercator, by Suzanne Hughes.

Al-Mar folder, by Oleg Volk.

Spyderco, by Suzanne Hughes.

Button-lock knife, by Suzanne Hughes.

Knife with thumb stud, by Suzanne Hughes.

Spyderco wave, by Oleg Volk.

Cutting a tube, before & after, by Casey Ferguson.

Cutting a rope, before & after, by Casey Ferguson.

Sparring Fairbairn-Sykes, by Suzanne Hughes.

Modified sparring knife, by Casey Ferguson.

Sparring Bowie, dagger and kukri, by Suzanne Hughes.

Kukri, HRC 42, by Suzanne Hughes.

Reinhardt combat kukri, HRC 649, by Suzanne Hughes.

WWII kukri, by Suzanne Hughes.

Small kukri, by Suzanne Hughes.

Cutting water bottle, by Kevin Gravitt.

Gladius, HRC 218, by Suzanne Hughes.

Jim Fikes Bowie blade, by Suzanne Hughes.

Bowie, HRC 129, from by Suzanne Hughes.

Historical Bowie, from *The Antique Bowie Knife Book*,
     reproduced by permission of Bill Adams.

Randall No. 1, by Suzanne Hughes.

Cutting newspaper, by Whit Williams.

Reproduction bronze dagger, HRC 175, by Suzanne
     Hughes.

Baselard, by Suzanne Hughes.

Main gauche, HRC 121, by Suzanne Hughes.

Randall No. 2 kit blade, by Suzanne Hughes.

Reproduction Fairbairn-Sykes, HRC 612, by Suzanne
     Hughes.

Randall No. 2, HRC 618, by Suzanne Hughes.

Jim Fikes Bowie with hilt, HRC 602, by Suzanne Hughes.